COUNSELING:

Offering a Needed Touch in Times of Trouble

A guide for personal care-giving

Major & Hoagland

Church Growth Institute

Providing Practical Tools for Growth

P.O. Box 4404, Lynchburg, VA 24502

Editor: Cindy G. Spear
Editorial and Design Assistant: Tamara Johnson
Cover Designer: James R. Copeland
Scriptures in this text are the King James Version of
the Holy Bible unless otherwise noted.

CONTENTS

INTRODUCTION

INTRODUCTION

Looking over the available books that deal specifically with care-giving in the church took very little time, simply because there are not many to read. Hence, we felt that a book on this subject, developed from the background and viewpoint of a full-time minister and a psychotherapist who is in private practice and ordained, would blend together to form a unique perspective that is biblically and psychologically sound.

This book is not intended to be an exhaustive study on the subject of care-giving in the church. Rather, it is designed to be an informative starting point for people interested in this specialized ministry to people. While it is true that there are thousands upon thousands of volumes on the subject of psychotherapy, psychology, and psychiatry, and there are thousands upon thousands of books, articles, and papers on topics that deal with ministering to people, our purpose in writing this book is to offer a practical application of topics that deal specifically with care-giving in the church. This book deals with common topics that concern both ministers and caregivers working with the pastor in their local church. Other books and readings on each chapter's topic are listed at the end of the text for your further reading and information.

Our unique blend of solid scriptural truths, coupled with sound psychological principle is presented in an easy to read and understand, practical format. We also added practical examples to many of the principles to bring about a better understanding of the principles shared. Above all, we pray that this book is a blessing to you, and that it will provide the practical information you need for a successful and meaningful ministry of care-giving.

CHAPTER ONE

CHAPTER ONE
A Brief Synopsis of Christian Counseling

The New Testament Church was a unique close-knit fellowship of believers. They cared for one another, helped each other in good and bad times, and were deeply involved in one another's lives. Yet, the New Testament itself is almost blank concerning the issues of counsel or giving advice.

As you study the Scriptures, you will find only a few examples of giving advice. Second Corinthians 8:10a: "And herein I give my advice..." and Acts 5:38-39: "And now I say unto you, refrain from these men, and let them alone: for if this counsel or this work be of men, it will come to nought."

The Old Testament views God's counsel as His fixed purpose. It was important that Israel, when facing national crises, received guidance from God. His Word provided instruction concerning the pattern of normal living. But when God's people faced crisis situations, the prophets often provided special counsel and advice (Amos 5:4-6).

The New Testament develops the theme of guidance. God wants to guide His people with His counsel. In the gospel of John we find Jesus' promise that He would return to God the Father, but He would send the Holy Spirit as Counselor (Greek – *parakletos*). Although the word *parakletos* has many shades of meaning, in this context the Spirit is seen as the One who interprets or counsels. Although the Spirit may use many ways to help us sense His direction, it is clear that the Spirit Himself takes on the role given to the Old Testament prophet. The Spirit guides us to decisions that are in harmony with what God purposes for us.

We live in a day and time when people are under maximum pressure. A pastor of a local church once said, "People stop us each day, and they repeat a similar phrase, 'Do you have a minute?' What they really mean is, 'Please give me some advice from a Christian perspective now.' If you are like most pastors, the first thought that runs through your mind is, 'When is there time to listen, care, and advise?' Then, your caring self kicks in and you respond, 'Sure, how about Tuesday night?' "

Scripture strongly suggests that Christians and pastors are called by God to be partners in the ministry of the church. That is the principle behind an Old Testament story found in Exodus 18:13-24. Moses' father-in-law suggested that Moses get some help with all the work he was doing because he knew that ministerial burn-out was close at hand. He advised Moses to delegate some responsibility to others. He realized that if Moses tried to do it all himself, he would completely burn-out and the people's needs would go unmet. Moses gave an ear to this advice and selected able leaders to help him in his tasks.

What was true for Moses is true of pastors today. We are not called to be "superpastors." If God wanted us to be this, He would have given us red boots, a blue jumpsuit and red cape! No pastor can lead the church, have time to prepare messages, proclaim the Gospel, and care for all the church membership alone. This is an impossible task even in a small church. When you add to this the pastor's need to have quiet time, time with his family, and time to be a regular human being, it is easy to see that no one person can do it all. Like Moses of old, modern-day pastors need help for the task they are called to do.

In reality, the entire church must be involved in carrying out the mission of the church. Every member must carry his or her weight. If God's work is to be accomplished, all must actively participate. Even when all members are doing their job, the pastor still needs special helpers. These special helpers, whose gifts are in the area of counseling and caring, become partners in ministry with the pastor. These Christians who are called to be servants of God assist in the direct work with people. Pastors need people who are trustworthy, caring, and who can work with others to create a type of pastoral team. This "team" is then able to meet the varied needs of the church and the church body in a shared ministry approach.

In writing this book, we realized that certain terms and words, although very familiar to us, are not familiar to others. Hence, to help you understand this book we felt it necessary to identify and define these terms here:

Lay Counselors – This term is for the non-professional people who counsel. They are not being paid for the counseling they do. This term does not speak of laity in the church.

Minister/Pastor – This person is a professional in that he is paid for performing the duties ascribed to the title. He is the one who performs redemptive, loving service for people in the Spirit of Christ.

Ministry – This is the act of performing redemptive, loving service for people in the Spirit of Christ both individually and as a church.

Care-giving Ministry – This ministry is set up in the local church, headed by the pastor, and enlists qualified (spiritually, educationally, experiencially) persons to minister through this ministry. It is not a professional "fee-for-service" undertaking, rather it is a ministry of the local church.

Probably every person who lives long enough will experience joy and grief, success and failure, hope and despair, health and sickness, life and death. Our world is filled with hurting people who need someone who will listen. They need someone to help them walk through the darkness and discover hope and light on the other side. They need someone to help them sort through numerous options and make healthy decisions about what to do in difficult situations. They need friends who will love them unconditionally. Unless you are unusual, you have experienced needs like this at some point in your life.

Hurting people need help. You can be a helping person, a caring person, a loving person, and a friend to people in need. This text will help you become the kind of counselor and caregiver you want to become. It is designed for Christians in the spiritual ministry of counseling. If you are concerned about your calling to this ministry, we suggest that you read Larry Gilbert's book entitled, *How to Find Meaning and Fulfillment through Understanding the Spiritual Gift within You.*[1] This book will be a great benefit in helping you discern and evaluate your gifts, and assess where your specific place in ministry is.

Many differences exist between secular counseling and "Christian" counseling. The chief difference between these two basic approaches is: "Christian" counseling (and I call it this because of the simpleness of the term), means that the counselor (or caregiver) has the mind of Christ and is guided by the Holy Spirit. He or she can provide sound spiritual counsel to hurting people. This spiritual ministry requires that a person be able to show the love of God in tangible ways through their ministry of care-giving. It also means that they must agree with God that they cannot effectively help others unless He works through them.

According to Ephesians 4:11-12, all of God's people are called to be involved in ministry. As a Christian, you are called and gifted for ministry in and through the body of Christ, the church.

The church's history includes many historical accounts of care-giving. None, however, are as poignant as an account from a church in Bristol, England, 1673.

"Our brother, John Fry, a bachelor, fell distracted. First it came upon him in a way of despairing, that he was lost and damned; then he brake out in bad language to all the brethren that came near him, calling them very bad names and immodest expressions to some women, raving and striking Christ, in them that came near to hold him, and when they were forced to bind him on the bed, he would spit at some, use such vile and grievous words, it was consternation of spirit to all that knew him, it being so directly opposite and contrary to the whole frame of his former way and temperament."

Most of the church members wanted to send Brother Fry to the country for help, but others proposed that the church hold a prayer vigil in his sickroom. So, on the morning of the fifth day of his illness, while he was still acutely disturbed, members of the church gathered in his room. Throughout the day, members of the church came and went, asking the Lord to heal their brother. Their prayers were answered. His rage left him "by the evening of that day before we parted from him. Praise be to the Lord!"

The illness was not quickly healed. When the rage left, the patient became fearful. Again the church responded with a day of intercessory prayer, followed by the standard medical treatment of the time, bleeding and purging. Fry improved enough to take some food. Then he became depressed and so ashamed of his behavior that he hid his eyes from visitors.

After the third day of prayer, Fry was strong enough to leave the house and go about his business for a few hours. The church clerk concluded the account with these words: "Praise the Lord! To God only be the glory! Whom, to this day, near three years since he recovered, the Lord hath kept in his former glorious frame of spirit...and hath been very well ever since in his body. Magnified be the Lord!"

The pastor at this time, Thomas Hardcastle, was "imprisoned seven times for religion." The record gives the impression that the church members themselves provided the pastoral care of Brother Fry supported by consultation from their pastor in prison! Wayne Oates, who visited the Broadmead church, pointed to this incident as an example of pastoral care based on the witness, instruction, and concern of the whole church.[2]

Care-giving has been at the center of the New Testament church's ministry from the local church in Ephesus until today. The uniqueness of our faith has been based on the two great commandments found in Matthew 22:37-40 "Jesus said unto him, Thou shalt love the Lord thy God with all thy heart, and with all thy soul, and with all thy mind. This is the first and great commandment. And the second is like unto it, Thou shalt love thy neighbour as thyself. On these two commandments hang all the law and the prophets." If this mandate of our Lord's is to be followed, then the implementation of a care-giving ministry is the obvious path. As you read this book, remain open to the Holy Spirit and his goal of empowering Christians to ministry.

The historical example of Brother Fry is interesting in its emphasis on collective prayer. It points to the great importance prayer has in the ministry of each and every caregiver. You will notice, however, that the account mentions that after a day of intercessory prayer the "standard medical treatment of the time" was followed. The account states that this medical treatment was "bleeding and purging," which is not the standard medical treatment of today. This does appear to speak, however, to the collaborative working of prayer and medical (and today, psychological) treatment.

Any care-giving that you do should be bathed in prayer. The emphasis of your praying should be directed two ways. First, toward you as a caregiver, for God's wisdom, understanding, and discernment before you get with the person(s) you are helping. Second, your praying should be about the person(s) you are to help. Your prayers should be both realistic (in your expectations) and specifically focused.

As mentioned in the definition of care-giving, you as a caregiver must be qualified spiritually, educationally, and experiencially according to the "treatment" of our time. This "treatment" speaks about your qualifications personally, and with your being able to enlist other treatments – be they medical or psychological – by referring the person(s) you are counseling when necessary. Actually, this format works very well. Pray for God's wisdom, direction, and discernment and know what you are doing and how much you can do. When you find that you are dealing with issues that you are not competent in or in areas that you are not comfortable with, refer them to someone qualified to help in those areas. Some time ago, I was seeing a 7-year-old boy. He had a problem with being able to leave his mother and would become very depressed when she was not in his immediate sight. Having had training in dealing with children, I worked with him and his mother. I thought that our progress was going well. He was able to go into another room with me and play, we were able to go into our parking lot where he rode his bicycle, all with his mother well out of sight. Toward the end of our fourth session, this young man began to go down hill right before my eyes when I suggested that we go and get a slushie drink. I knew that the progress we had made was not helping him to the degree I had thought and that someone else with more training and experience than I would be better for him. I suggested to his mother that he be referred to a woman in our practice, and explained my concerns. She was very willing, as was the therapist, and they began sessions together. About a month later, I saw the boy's mother in our waiting room. I casually asked her how things were going for her and her son. What she told me I will not soon forget. "He is really making progress. I want to thank you so much for referring him. When I first came to your office, I was very leery about counselors in general. I thought that all they wanted to do was take my money. But by you referring my son, I have confidence in counselors that they really do want to help and that they are not just out for the money. Thank you so much."

While prayer is foundational to any care-giving intervention, it does not usually take the place of other "treatments" working in conjunction with it. Many ministers will tell a person to "throw away all your medications and turn it over to Jesus." While I would agree that they should turn to God and pray for His guidance and healing, I would never agree that the person should throw away all their medications if in fact they are necessary. One woman I was seeing in treatment some time ago had a very difficult time with depression and bizarre thinking. She had attempted suicide a number of times before her medications were started. It was necessary for her to be on a regular anti-depressant so that she could sleep and think straight. "A minister," she said, "told me to throw away all my pills and ask for God to heal me." If she would have followed his advice, it is very likely that she would not be here today. But because of our therapy relationship, which included prayer and treatment, she was able to see her daughter graduate, and be an influential part in helping her get into a Christian college.

Other treatments should not take the place of strong effectual prayer. They work hand-in-hand; prayer, treatment, and more prayer. Any therapist who is a Christian will tell you that without prayer for God's wisdom and guidance in their treatment of the people they see, their task of helping is very difficult at best. You need both. One without the other does not produce the ability for timely healing.

FOOTNOTES

1 Gilbert, Larry. *How to Find Meaning and Fulfillment through Understanding the Spiritual Gift within You*. (Church Growth Institute, 1987).

2 Hightower, James E., compiler. *Called to Care: Helping People Through Pastoral Care* (Convention Press, Nashville, TN, 1990).

CHAPTER TWO

CHAPTER TWO
Uniqueness of Christian Counseling

Just because a person claims the name of Christ, they are not necessarily a Christian. Likewise, those who call themselves *counselors* may not be people who are capable, trained or qualified to be counselors. I have been a born-again believer in Jesus Christ for over 20 years. Just because I have a personal relationship with Christ does not make me a Christian counselor. On the other hand, a person who has a Bible in their office, or uses a few Scriptures in their counseling sessions, is not necessarily a Christian counselor.

Where I'm from, Christian counseling has come to mean something that is second rate, uneducated, and impoverished as to sound theory and practice. Basically, people believe that if you have a small, everyday problem, you go to the "Christian counselor." If you have a long-standing or "deep emotional problem," you don't see a "Christian counselor;" you see a "professional" who has better training. I think that this is a shame, and do not believe that this pervasive attitude is necessarily true, but I am forced to live within the mental images this term gives to people in the area I live. This idea is not only prevalent in my small city. There appears to be a question in many cities as to the qualifications of Christian counselors.

I do not tell people that I am a Christian counselor. Rather, I tell them that I am a Christian who counsels professionally. I am a born-again believer, an ordained minister, and I have the academic training, state license, and national certifications to practice in the areas of interest and manner I choose. I often attend training seminars to stay current with specific areas of practice, and conduct workshops and training programs for various groups.

When I tell this to people who are contemplating therapy, they seem to understand. They know of the qualifications and training I have and are comfortable with them. If they are concerned as to whether they are talking to a Christian counselor, my explanation that I am a Christian who is an ordained minister and licensed professional counselor pleases most of them.

As I stated before, what counts is not what you advertise yourself to be, rather it is what you do and how you conduct yourself. How you view people, their problems, and what you hold as a guideline for dealing with the many problems people present to you in counseling is of utmost importance. It is also necessary to be informed about basic counseling theory and technique, and to embrace one theory as your "home base" point of operation. This home base is of course secondary to the Scriptures.

There is no reason why you, as a Christian who wants to help others through the medium of counseling, should be ill-informed or ignorant as to the use of God's Word in counseling. Assuming that you are qualified spiritually and personally, you need to qualify yourself educationally to be the best you can be, the most knowledgeable you can be, to do the job God has called you to do. If you are not willing to learn, be trained, and work at your identity as a counselor, you should first check your calling. Making yourself available to be a counselor in your church, or thinking about establishing a caregiving ministry in your church, requires dedication and direction from God. If either are not there, neither should you be!

A few years ago, I was in charge of organizing and running a large pastor/layperson one-week seminar that taught Christians how to counsel others. The seminars averaged well over 400 people in attendance, which went on yearly, for four years. Most people who attended were not professionals, though some were. All were interested in helping others and finding out various biblical techniques to do their job better. It seemed that most of these people were anxious and hungry to learn more about the practical application of God's Word to human problems. They wanted more than just someone spouting out a few Scriptures, much like a Band-Aid™. Rather, they wanted a practical, spelled out understanding and appropriate application of the Scriptures for people who are hurting. They needed something that the hurting person could take with them to their situation and have the Holy Spirit work with them through the hurt to a healing resolve.

A number of good, sound materials have been written in the last decade which strive to clarify the Scriptures in a practical and applicable manner to meet the needs of people where they live. Dr. Jay Adams has long been involved with training, speaking, and counseling others in this manner. He has written numerous books which, whether you agree with them or not, have helped people better understand what Christian counseling is, along with practical techniques of using the Scriptures in counseling. Dr. Gary Collins and Dr. Larry Crabb have also written many articles and books, along with speaking around the country on the topic of Christian counseling. They have made materials available that instruct people in the church how to counsel in a practical and easy-to-understand manner.

Personally, my "home-base" theory is wrapped in what is called a cognitive or behavioral approach to counseling. The word *cognitive* lends itself to how a person thinks. The word *behavioral* deals with how a person behaves or acts; what they do. The Bible talks about these two modes of operation: "For as he thinketh in his heart, so is he" (Prov. 23:7a). Behaviorally, we are admonished to walk the walk, not just talk the talk.

While it is true that some people will see only the pastor, and some situations will require that the pastor be personally "on the job," not all will require "only the pastor's attention." Personally, I believe that key lay-people in the church can immensely help the pastor and the church body as a whole – especially in the area of counseling others. Dr. Gary Collins has presented in numerous publications, a basic and more in-depth understanding of Christian care-giving (lay counseling). We will discuss this topic in further detail, along with some of the issues that surround a definition of care-giving, how to select caregivers, and training caregivers.

As mentioned earlier, all who claim to be Christians, or all who claim to be Christian counselors, are not necessarily what they seem. If you are sure of your spiritual calling to be an active helper in your church to people in need, let me explain the uniqueness to which you have been called. The uniqueness I will explain does not exempt you from knowing basic ethical standards. It does not allow you to not have a complete understanding of the boundaries you must operate within when helping others. Nor does it give you a license to be ignorant of sound psychological principles or "people" skills. Rather, it does require that you implement these, and others, to the highest degree of your ability when you exercise your calling to help others in need.

Christians who are called to be caregivers using the Bible as their basic presupposition for understanding the human condition, have a number of unique underpinnings that tend to separate their task from a non-Christian-oriented foundation. I will explain some of these unique underpinnings I believe are important to an understanding of why using the Bible as your foundation to care-giving is important.

1. The Total Person. Counseling people in need from a biblical perspective requires an accurate knowledge about the nature of man. You must have an accurate perspective which deals with the total person, not just specific portions of their makeup. People are made up of body, soul, and spiritual dimensions which need to be addressed when dealing with issues that affect their success in dealing with life's situations. Body, speaks to our physical representation. There is an inseparable link that binds our body with our soul, or emotional dimension. Many physicians recognize this link when dealing with the medical aspects of their patients. They realize that the turmoil and strains that affect us emotionally (or mentally), tend to carry over and affect us physically. Stress is a common example that most of us can relate to. When we emotionally feel stress in our lives, whether actual or perceived, it sets off the same reactions in our bodies that being chased by a pit-bull would. Various chemicals in our bodies change, our heart-rate increases as does our blood pressure. Breathing becomes shallow and oxygen rich, and blood is diverted from the intestinal regions of our bodies into major muscle groups to ready them for action. There are a number of other physiological changes that come about in a fraction of a second when faced with stress. This all comes "standard-issue" from God, and is a way that we can preserve our lives. Truly when a real danger is facing us, it is comforting to know that our bodies will automatically function in such a way so as to get us to safety if at all possible.

The problem comes when your body starts to change, as though ready for fight or flight, and you are sitting in a comfortable chair watching an old movie. You should be relaxing, but because of some emotional "stress" that bombards you, your body is ready to go, and you begin to feel that you are ready to go....to the hospital. The opposite is also true – when we physically feel bad or sick, our emotional state is many times compromised. Think of the last time you were really sick. High temperature, nauseated, and feeling in desperate need of staying in bed. Right when you are ready to call it a day and go home and crawl (maybe literally) into bed, someone has to see you. Even if you are able to limit your time to just talking to them on the phone, your emotions are strained. Maybe you find yourself getting upset over things that usually wouldn't bother you, but because you feel so terrible, they do. So, as you can see, and as you have probably experienced yourself, your mind and emotions (or body and soul) are linked together and do affect one another in some very dramatic ways. The third dimension, that many people leave out when they counsel people, is the spiritual dimension. This also is affected by the other two dimensions that make up a person. When you feel sick physically (body), you are usually more touchy emotionally (soul) which affects your spiritual talk, walk, or thinking. If you are emotionally (soul) all caught up in wrong thinking, which leads to wrong feelings also, then your physical health may be compromised as well as your spiritual effectiveness and abilities.

Many theories of counseling leave out this spiritual aspect of man. For when the spiritual aspect is out of balance with the other two dimensions, there is a two-legged stool (rather than a three-legged stool) effect that is not balanced very well. So unstable is it that it is certain to get knocked out of balance when pressure pushes it one way, then another, then still another. By addressing and understanding the integration of the spiritual dimension (or the third leg of the three-legged stool) of a person's life, you are able to balance the third leg of the stool. When in balance, the person is able to better withstand the many strains and pressures life gives to us. The tossing and turning of life may wiggle them some, but will not turn them over. They are not so easily toppled over because they have all three legs on the floor – body, soul, and spirit – all holding the person solidly through whatever situation may come about. This unison is the perspective that the Bible offers in our viewing man from a health perspective.

In dealing with the total person, the Scriptures also give us an accurate understanding about the nature of man. Scripture teaches that man was created in God's image, but is incomplete until he gets into a proper relationship with God through a personal relationship with Christ. Hence, counseling that ignores man's spiritual need is not dealing with the whole person. Man's nobility comes from his being created in God's image, but his depravity comes from the fall and his alienation from God.

2. A Healthy Personality Perspective. The Scriptures also deal with counseling others from a perspective of health, rather than from a picture of deviancy. The picture we have of health is Christ himself. We are growing through the experiences of life to be "conformed to the image of his Son" (Rom. 8:29). God uses situations that He allows to come into our lives to teach us things that no other situation could ever teach us. We know what we are striving for in the picture we have of Christ. There are numerous examples of how to deal with various situations we face from a healthy perspective. One example may serve well to emphasize this point. Many people, especially Christian people, believe that is it wrong to even have the emotion of anger. They believe that it is wrong and sinful to even acknowledge this God-given emotion. Yes, I said God-given! Anger IS a God-given emotion that can make life more interesting. We were not allowed to have this emotion without having the ability to exercise it some! When Christ "turned to the money-changers" in the temple, He probably did not have a smile on His face. The emotion of anger was a part of His being and was expressed toward how the temple was changed to a "den of thieves." The

Bible tells us that "He cast out all them that sold and bought in the temple and overthrew the tables of the money changers" (Matt. 21:12-16). The Bible tells us that God is angry with the wicked every day (Ps. 7:11). A healthy person is one who can experience anger. The question is not whether you can experience anger but the way it affects your subsequent actions. The Bible tells us to "be ye angry and sin not" (Eph. 4:26). So it is not a problem to have experienced the emotion of anger. In fact, we may go so far as to suggest that it is a healthy emotion to experience, as long as you do not allow it to to be coupled with actions of anger. When people think of anger, they picture the emotion of anger and the action of anger together. In actuality, these are two different things. As stated, the emotion of anger is actually healthy. It is a God-given emotion. The subsequent angry actions, that most people tie together with the emotion, is what causes a problem for most of us. Yes, it is very possible to have the emotions of anger without expressing the actions of anger with it. Holding the emotions inside and putting on a (pseudo) smile is not the answer. There are other ways to release or express anger.

Jennifer was very upset about her friend not being able to come over at the last minute. They had planned their get together for a week, and 15 minutes before the friend was to come to Jennifer's house, she called and said that "something had come up." Jennifer had looked forward to being with her friend, and was very angry that she was not able to get together as they had planned. Rather than throw things around and break them, she decided to vent her anger in another, more positive fashion. She remembered other times when she had been angry. Yelling at people close to her, slamming down items that weren't made to be handled in a rough manner and subsequently breaking them, along with a host of other ways she had acted when angry that had not worked very well for her in the past. "This time is going to be different," she thought. She was very angry but needed to do something different with her expression of anger. So, she decided to take a long, fast walk around the block. Jennifer walked faster than she normally would. She allowed the anger to slowly slip away through her walking. When she returned to her home, after walking a number of times around the block, she recognized that her anger was gone. Sure, she was still disappointed that the plans to get together with her friend were shot, but the anger generated from that information was not displayed in an adverse manner. Jennifer actually used the anger she had to propel her around the block a number of times. A by-product of this anger was that she also was getting a good exercise workout too!

3. A Source of Authority. Christians who counsel have a tremendous authority at their disposal...the Word of God! The standard for a picture of mental health, and an infinite source of knowledge from the guidance of the Holy Spirit, also comes from God's Word. Because of your relationship with Christ, YOU have available this power, insight, and boldness to share the Scriptures with people who come to you for help and in need of the HOPE that is theirs through a proper alignment with Christ and His teachings. Your position as a caregiver puts you in the unique position to rightly discern the truth (2 Tim. 2:15b), and to help wrong thinking and beliefs. You are able to share biblical truths along specific guidelines which enables you to speak with confidence, boldness, and direction.

4. A Unique Goal. The goal you as a caregiver have when dealing with people who come to you for help is more than alleviating their immediate problem. When you deal with crisis issues, you will want to focus on the immediate problem and strive to channel their energies into a productive course (see Chap. 9, for a more complete discussion about crisis intervention). When talking to people in a non-crisis setting, your goal is to assist the person in taking steps toward becoming more like Christ. Becoming more like Christ, our unique picture of a healthy personality, is a direction toward emotional and spiritual health also. Because of the physical dimension, a significant amount of physical healing may take place also when these other two dimensions are strengthened.

The aim of this unique goal, as previously stated, is to become more like Christ. It is not enough to act like Christ, because sometimes people get so caught up in showing others, by their actions, that they are Christlike, that they fail. They fail because rather than having the Christlike attitudes and behaviors flowing out of them toward others from deep inside their own being, they "manufacture" a pseudo-Christlikeness for a number of other reasons, none of which are usually honoring to God!

5. Supernatural Power and Guidance. Through the indwelling power of the Holy Spirit, the caregiver has a source of knowledge, understanding, and guidance (John 14:26) that enables him or her to be more effective in helping others. The combined power and authority of God's Word and the Holy Spirit affords the caregiver a power far beyond human ability. The concept to visualize here is not one of a "coaching" relationship. Rather, the idea is one of a "player/coach" relationship. The Holy Spirit does not just lead you into doing things that are supposed to work; He guides you, through His leading, in ways that have been experienced already! Note that this is available to any believer who allows God to work through them, but is sharply limited when we get in the way of what God wants to do through us.

6. A Unique Love for the Individual. You as a caregiver allowing God to work through you, can share and show the love of God to a hurting person. The ability to reflect God's love and concern in addition to your own personal concern for the person(s) you counsel may be the only visible representation of God's love and concern for them and their situation that they see. Remember that you may be seeing people who are new to your church. You may counsel, in your capacity as a caregiver, people who outwardly do all the Christian things, (walk the walk and talk the talk) but inwardly have not had a personal relationship with Christ. The situation that brings them to you may be their first experience with the practical application of God's love and concern for them and their situation. This situation may also bring them to a saving relationship with God. No other situation has done this to date, except this one for which you are seeing them about. And, you as a caregiver have the opportunity to demonstrate, in a practical, representative way, the willingness and ability for God to meet their needs, where they live, and in a way that demonstrates that the practical application of godly principles to their lives really does work!

7. A God-Dependency. It is very easy for hurting people to overly depend upon the one who is helping them. Their dependency does not need to be upon you! If your need is to foster this type of dependence, you will go a long way in hurting the person who is trusting you for help. You may even do more harm than what could have been done by your not seeing them.

The Christian caregiver needs to encourage the person to build a dependency upon God, not upon the caregiver. You as a caregiver need to demonstrate this dependency in your own life so that when you encourage them to depend upon God, your life will be an example. Do not trust in gimmicks, self-power, etc. Rather, let your dependency upon God and His leading be so evident that you need not verbally tell them of it. It should show through your verbal and non-verbal behaviors in such a way that you don't need to verbally tell others... They'll see it for themselves.

Susan and Bob were going through a really tough time in their marriage. Actually, it wasn't their marriage that was the problem, it was the pressures of parenting a teenage daughter that was testing the strength of their marriage. Bob was a caregiver in their local church, and had talked to a number of people who were having similar situations with their children. Bob's daughter was going to a party with a friend for the first time. Both Bob and Susan were concerned whether or not she would uphold the values they had taught her by both word and deed. Yes, they could have told her not to go, or they could have made up some excuse for stopping by the place she and her friend were going to. Instead, they decided to commit her to the Lord, and trust her that she would adhere to the values she was taught. They were also concerned about her being home on time. After all, this was their daughter's first time to a get together with school friends, and the first time for Mom and Dad to have their daughter go out! When she got home, she told them of one person who offered her some beer and about how she declined the offer. The friend she went with wanted to go to another party, then go out to eat. Because she wanted to get home on time, she told the friend to just drop her off on their way. She was proud of herself for sticking to principles she had been taught and believed in. Bob and Susan were both thankful and proud of her actions too. All-in-all, their daughter's first outing was a very successful one. The statement their daughter made to them was perhaps the highlight of the evening when she said, "Dad, I remembered what you told me about hanging around the wrong crowd. I didn't know that there would be drinking at this party but I figured that since you and Mom have always been straight with me, and neither of you drink, that it wasn't for me either."

This dependency upon God is a "trust" relationship that is independent of external crutches but depends upon the Lord. Hence, your capacity as a caregiver is that of a growth facilitator. Assist your clients in removing hindrances in their life that prevent them from developing and trusting in Christ. Teach them to find, both in the Bible and in their relationship with God, strength, hope, and comfort for every situation they face. Teach them to call upon God (at any time of the night or day) (Ps. 1:2) rather than having to call you whenever they have questions or are in need of guidance.

8. A Unique Model. Having the Scriptures as a guideline for living and dealing with the many problems that face us in our daily lives, it is important that the caregiver demonstrate in his or her personal life the qualities he or she is espousing to the people with problems. When someone comes to you for a problem that is taking control of their life and this area of trouble is also a weak spot in your life, potential problems can arise quickly. An example of this is you seeing someone who is having trouble with finances. It is not so much a problem, you soon understand, that they do not have the money to pay their bills as much as it is that they are routinely late with payments, obligations, etc. This may also be a tip-off that other areas of their life are disorganized and chaotic as well. It would be reasonable to investigate whether or not there are other areas of this person's life that they are "late" with also. Let's say, for example, you find they are late for work and appointments more times than not. Clearly, prioritizing their time and talents is something you would need to bring up. Assisting them with a routine, schedule, and so forth may help greatly.

All of the assistance you give, no matter how good, will be greatly diminished if you yourself are always late for your scheduled appointments with them. If, in your personal life, you are not able to put into practice what you are telling others they should do, you not only discredit your word, but the Word of God. There are many examples of people who say one thing and do another. Sometimes this happens by mistake. But, there are many who "play the part" but do not have the substance to genuinely be able to say "this is what I have done."

You see, Christ was able to tell his followers, "Therefore, whosoever heareth these sayings of mine, and doeth them..." (Matt. 7:24) because He was a living example of what He expected them to do, and how He expected them to act. He was an example before their eyes in a variety of situations; some joyful (John 2:11); some sorrowful (John 11: 33-35), and some in the midst of having everything "humanly" looking as if it were going all wrong (at His crucifixion – Luke 22:42). Yet, throughout all of these situations and emotional experiences, Christ showed them an example of how to act, talk, and think. He encouraged them by His exemplary life how to live successfully and not be tossed and turned by others in situations they had no control over. He wanted them to be grounded (2 Tim. 2:15), staying consistent (Prov. 25:19) in their personal life so that they too could be an example to others about how to live and deal with any circumstance successfully (2 Cor. 1:6).

The apostle Paul was so dedicated to Christ and determined to live his life above reproach that he could say, "Be ye followers of me, even as I also am of Christ" (1 Cor. 11:1). This is not to say that Paul was perfect, and never did any wrong after he was saved. Rather, it suggests that his relationship with God was so strong that his actions and attitudes changed drastically. This change was not to please men, rather it was from a complete dedication to God, His will and direction for Paul's life. His life so changed that he could use his life as an example for others to follow.

9. A Unique Attitude Toward the Past. No one can live a successful life and ignore their past. The saying, "We are the sum total of our past," is true. Everything that has happened to you, every experience you have gone through, and the corresponding attitudes and beliefs you hold have been developed from your collective experiences, both good and bad.

While it is true that you cannot forget the past, though many of us would like to "edit" some parts out of our past experiences, our past does not have to have control over us. What has happened in our collective past has made us what we are right now. It happened for a reason. Hopefully we can learn from our past mistakes so that we can be more successful in the future. However, this is not always the case.

Romans 8:28 gives us the message of forgiveness which enables us to leave our sins and mistakes at the Cross. If you can demonstrate this attitude toward the past to people who come to you for help, it will allow them to gain a unique perspective of how everything that has happened in their life is for a purpose. God has allowed various experiences to happen to them to mold and shape them into a person who can exemplify the person of Christ more fully. Therefore, they can come to see that rather than "editing" parts of their past, they can give thanks for the things that have happened to bring them closer to the conformity of Christ (1 Thess. 5:18).

Years ago, I went into a business venture with three other men. We were all Christians, and were honestly trying to put God first in what we were doing. We worked hard in our various capacities to get this business off the ground, to "feed" it during the proceeding months of questionable stability. In the end, all of us lost tens of thousands of dollars, and the business failed. When I opened up my private practice, a different venture than this last one, I was very nervous. I looked back on the past efforts, and decided that I had better be very careful with this new undertaking because I did not want to repeat the failure. I found some very valuable experiences that helped me to be successful. In the first venture, I did not know much about the workings of a restaurant. I was not trained in the management or workings of a restaurant, nor did I desire to be a full-time restauranteer. I was in over my head (knowledge and training wise), but thought that since we were all Christians who wanted to honor Christ in our business, that my lack of knowledge and training would be "overlooked." Secondly, and perhaps most importantly, I learned that just because I lost a lot of time and money in the restaurant, I should not be afraid to make a decision to open a private practice. After all, I was trained in theology and psychology, and I wanted to be a full-time counselor. Thirdly, I realized that my mistake with the restaurant was good. I had learned to not be a part of something I knew little (or nothing) about, and that God had allowed me to fail to better understand this truth. After over 10 years in private practice (having started three successful private practices myself), I can honestly say that the lessons learned from that "failure" were the lessons I needed to learn so that I could be successful in what I do now. If I had not learned these lessons, I believe that my choice to start a private counseling practice would have been wrought with many more problems and possible failures. The bottom line is that I learned from my experiences. The learning experience was expensive in both time and money but if I had not learned the lessons God wanted me to learn there, I would have made them in my private practice. Maybe the learning experience would have been more difficult if I had not listened and learned from the failed restaurant experience.

The past then can be used as a tool for teaching and understanding rather than serving as a dumping ground for blame or as an excuse for avoiding personal responsibility. God expects everyone to live responsibly in the present and not blame experiences in the past.

10. A Unique Methodology. The various principles of successful living are given in the Scriptures. But, the process of applying or sharing with others is not detailed. Though I would like to believe that God has a special blessing for those who use a cognitive-behavioral approach to care-giving, I cannot say that it is true. At times, a very directive approach is best to use. At other times, a more passive and bonding type of approach is needed. Still at other times, especially when a loved one has just died, a more silent and reflective approach is what is needed. There is NO scriptural method for care-giving! But, there are scriptural absolutes that must be recognized and honored, whatever the method is. As mentioned before, it is important that you have a "home-base" theoretical perspective that is psychologically sound. This does not replace or come before your biblical perspective, and should not conflict at all. Again, we can look to the Scriptures for guidelines of how to practice care-giving.

Jesus, for example, talked personally with people. He touched some, cried with others, rebuked some, and confronted others. Often when He spoke with people, He did so in a very direct manner. However, He never wrote letters.

Paul shared his life with many, admonished others, taught some, and wrote many letters. He detailed his methodology in 1 Thess. 5:14, which stated: "Now we exhort you, brethren, warn them that are unruly, comfort the feebleminded, support the weak, be patient toward all men."

Hence, it appears that the Christian caregiver must maintain Scriptural absolutes. But, there are certain freedoms in the application and methods by which you choose to give care. Perhaps an understanding of your personal spiritual gifts would help you better understand how God has made you so that you can be the most effective caregiver possible. A Christian who uses his or her gifts to the maximum efficiency receives a minimum amount of fatigue and frustration.

CHAPTER THREE

CHAPTER THREE
What Did the Pastor Have in Mind?

Carrington was both surprised and somewhat shocked when his pastor approached him after the Wednesday night service. "Carrington, our church is starting a care-giving ministry soon. I know that in your college and graduate courses, you have had quite a lot of counseling and psychology classes and I would like for you to consider being on the care-giving team. A lot of training will be involved and I believe that your reputation in the church and your spiritual maturity as a leader in the church would be a great asset to this ministry. Prayerfully consider this ministry, and let me know your decision next week."

Let me share with you some of the thoughts that may have been going through your pastor's mind when he asked YOU to be a caregiver in your church. Your pastor has realized that no one Christian has a monopoly on giving counsel or advice to people in need. True, there are certain situations where only the pastor will do to talk to. But, there are many other times and situations where a solid, trained, spirit-led layperson within the church body can help others in need as well. Quite possibly, your pastor is trying to accomplish two things at once. One, he wants to give an opportunity of service to people in his congregation who have specific training and talents. His thought in asking you for this ministry suggests that he thinks you possess the training, knowledge, and spiritual gifts along with good common sense and a positive track record for a care-giving ministry. Secondly, it is a wise decision on his part to have people in the congregation help in ministering to the body so that his time and talent is better focused on tasks that only he can perform. Remember that your pastor needs time to study the Word of God and prepare messages that feed and edify the people. He also needs personal time to be a husband and father too! Perhaps his interest in starting a care-giving ministry and his asking you to partake in this ministry is a wise decision on his part in maximizing the talents of the church for the edification of the body. It also suggests that your pastor is not stuck in the idea that "only the pastor can give spiritual counsel." Many times, pastors are reluctant to allow anyone else to help others. They feel that it is their job, and only their job, to be a caregiver to their congregation. Sometimes this attitude is born from a lot of insecurity. Other times, it is fostered by a need to control everything that is done. Whatever the reason, your pastor appears to be secure enough in both his calling and his knowledge of his own personal time limitations to seek other qualified individuals to work with him in ministering to the church through the medium of caregiving.

Your pastor did not ask you to be a caregiver in order to inflate your head to the point that you can't fit into the sanctuary. His idea is not to develop a little "click" of spiritual persons who are better than other people. This is not "The Pastor's Club," nor is it a grouping of people who laud their being asked to serve over others. Remember that your pastor is the head servant to his people. Your ministry as a caregiver is an extension of his ministry. In other words, having a pompous, better-than-thou attitude has no place in this ministry. Your pastor has asked you to serve in this ministry to help others, not to become unapproachable or "special" because you meet with the pastor.

Your pastor has chosen to approach you, and others, after much prayer and consideration of your training, strengths and abilities. Yes, you have a right to be proud that God has directed him to ask you, but be proud that God has seen fit to have you serve others in this capacity. This type of "proudness" is evidenced in a meek and mild spirit; in an attitude of serving and helping others; in a behavior that is approachable to those hurting and in need of a caregiver. It is amazing to me how so many people want to be cared about. So many seek recognition through behaviors that draw attention (whether good or bad) to themselves. They want someone to care about them as an individual, to help them go through the various trials and tribulations that life offers. And most of all, they need someone to help them learn from the experiences that God has allowed them to go through so that they become more closely conformed to the image of Christ. You, as a caregiver, are in this unique position to help facilitate change in other people's lives. Your life can be a stumbling block to this change, or it can be a vehicle by which people God allows to come in contact with you can look back upon and say, "without their help in showing me God's plan for my life, I don't know where I would be today." What greater reward, what greater "payment" could you receive than for someone's life to be changed for the better because you were there as a caregiver to help them in their hour of need?

As Carrington contemplated these and other thoughts as to "WHY" his pastor asked him to be a caregiver in the church, it gave him a sense of peace and understanding. He knew the answer to "WHY," and was thankful to God for allowing him to have the opportunity to help others by assisting them in their growth and development as believers. He felt a sense of honor and dedication to the task before him. He knew that this ministry was not just something to jump into, rather it was a huge responsibility that could not be taken lightly. His wife and family were supportive of his decision to tell the pastor that he would serve, and his prayers were answered toward this decision he had made.

Carrington went on to receive the care-giving training that his pastor had set up. The information he had received in his college classes that dealt with counseling and specific topics the pastor covered added to this training. His pastor arranged for people with a lot of training and knowledge to speak and train them also. Some of them were professionals in full-time counseling work and some were trained in specialized areas. This training reminded Carrington of the hard work and dedication this ministry needed. It also helped him to better understand the significance of prayer and the Word of God in this ministry. He remembered the admonition that stated "study to show thyself approved unto God" (2 Tim. 2:15). Many hours of reading and self-examination were logged through the training time. Carrington also remembered that the key to being a supportive caregiver had much to do with something that was hard for many to do...listen to others. So many times we think we have to jump through rings to be successful. Time after time God just wants us to be available and willing to be used of the Holy Spirit.

Carrington is a powerful witness to others, and is known as someone who is not only knowledgeable, but as someone who really cares about people. He and the other caregivers in the church have been called upon many times when it was inconvenient, and a few times when it seemed down-right impossible for them to help. But, through much prayer, God's direction, and a sense of working together, they have made a difference in many people's lives. Potentially broken homes have been mended to where they are stronger than before. People whose lives were shattered were put back together. One person is singing in the choir today instead of playing a harp in heaven, just because Carrington's pastor asked him to be a caregiver. Carrington's training and dedication to this ministry, and his proper understanding of his ministry has made a change in many people's lives. Many can say, "I don't know where I'd be today if that person had not touched my life."

CHAPTER FOUR

CHAPTER FOUR
Knowing Your Limitations

One of the problems that seems to plague many people is not knowing their personal and professional limitations. This gets people into a lot of trouble in a number of ways.

Some people will make a statement or do something in which they are not really knowledgeable. Usually, after a brief period of time, they realize that what they said or did was not correct. Other people seem to have a definite flaw in their understanding of their abilities and knowledge. You probably know of someone or have at least heard of the person who always has a definite opinion on everything. They are the first ones to put in their 5 cents worth whether asked to do so or not. Some with this ability actually do know "something" about the subject at hand, but are not well versed enough to thoroughly know much about what they are talking about.

While we all know someone who would fit into one of these categories, it is very important that the Christian caregiver fully understand his or her knowledge and abilities when helping others. Accurate knowledge of your strengths and limitations are essential in four areas. Specifically, they are your (1) Personal life, (2) Professional life, (3) Public life, and (4) Private life.

Personal Life: This is foundational to all other areas because it is the foundation that threads through the other areas. If my personal life is out of control, or if I do not fully understand what my strengths and abilities are, it will be almost impossible to know what my limitations are.

Bob was a trained caregiver in his local church. A church member was referred to him, by the pastor, who shared that she and her husband were having trouble with their 13-year-old. Bob welcomed the referral and set up a meeting time to see the child. The problem was that Bob did not have any experience in working with adolescents. To further the problem, Bob and his wife had two children of their own they were having trouble with, neither of which were over the age of 5. True, Bob could personally relate to having small children, and to having two children, but he could not personally relate to the various dynamics going on with an adolescent.

When we talk about limitations, we are not talking about personality flaws, nor are we talking about some other character deficiencies. Rather, we are identifying the abilities that God has given us and ones that He has allowed us to develop through adversity and situations that have helped shape who we are right now. Bob and his wife were going through what most couples experience when they have two children under the age of 5 years: a lot of turmoil, a lot of adjusting, and an almost constant feeling of frustration and loss of energy. Just because Bob did not have an adolescent of his own *did not* disqualify him from seeing this adolescent. Rather, his inability to get control of the situation in his own home with his own family was the problem. As Bob thought about it, he began to better understand how parenting was a very difficult task. He remembered what good parents he and his wife thought they would be before they had children of their own. "How could it all have changed so dramatically" he often thought. Another plaguing thought Bob entertained was, "If I can't make sense out of my role as a parent with my own kids, what am I doing trying to help others with their kids?" It makes little sense to try and help others straighten out their lives when your own life feels like an out-of-control roller coaster.

Professional Life: For the minister, being able to meet the needs of the church is paramount. However, most congregations believe that the pastor should be available any time, no matter when! As mentioned in Chapter One, a minister commonly gives up whatever free time he has when asked to talk with someone. Personally, I believe there are times that are not convenient for the pastor to talk with someone but the situation requires it. However, I also believe that all too often the "need" to talk right now is not actually justified.

Reverend Lee was a true man of God. His congregation loved him and he was always able to deliver a timely sermon that seemed to meet the needs of his congregation. It seemed as though he was at every function that went on in the church. After attending a seminar with his wife, Reverend Lee decided that he would put into practice what he and his wife had learned; spend time with self, with each other, and with their family. He remembered how he was sick much of the time, was constantly fatigued, and how even his physician had told him that he needed to slow down. The implementation of their plan, to spend time on self, with each other, and with family worked fine while they were away for the weekend following the end of the retreat. When they returned home, the phone began to ring as soon as they came in the door. The same thing was happening that had threatened both his health and his relationship with his wife and family before...having phone calls at all hours of the day and night, people "dropping by" without warning, and people "expecting" him to be at the church whenever the doors were open. It seemed as though all they had learned was lost, and the same old patterns were starting up fast.

A concept I share with patients I see in therapy is called "healthy selfish." It involves taking care of yourself some, and is based on the belief that if I do not spend a little "healthy" time on myself, I soon will be completely depleted and unable to help others. There is scriptural evidence of Christ taking time to be by Himself (Mark 14:32-42; Luke 22: 39-43) to pray and re-group. Even in highly energized competition situations (football, basketball, boxing, etc.) these "professionals" take a little time for themselves to re-group, plan, and rest. We call these times "time-outs," "half-times," or end of "rounds." If it is important for these professionals to take occasional "breaks" from what they are doing, it should be for pastors who are "on the field" and in front of the "home audience" all the time to take them too. "Healthy selfish" also speaks to the idea of doing something that is good for you personally. The time spent here should not rob your wife or family of their needed time with you, but it may include time with them where you can relax, enjoy, and not be under so much pressure.

If you do not have the time to get with someone who wants to talk with you as a caregiver, or if the time needed to get with them will involve a large amount of time over a long period, it is a "healthy selfish" thing to consider referring them to someone who can devote the amount of time their situation requires. Reverend Lee started telling the people who wanted to talk with him: "Your situation certainly sounds involved. It seems that with what you have shared with me, it would be best for Mr. Jones to get with you on a regular basis. He works with me in situations like yours, and is very skilled in helping people. I believe that he would be able to devote the time your situation requires and the support you need, to give you the help you need. With your permission, I will have him (or her) contact you tomorrow." Reverend Lee found that in most cases, when he stated that he would not be able to spend the time required and offered an alternative, the person was satisfied. You may want to attend the first session to introduce the person to Mr. Jones. Showing your support for his ability both verbally and visually with your presence will usually abate any fears or concerns the person has.

For laypeople, the "healthy selfish" concept still applies. You are employed at a job which requires you to work the best you can during the time required. You also, like the pastor, need to have quality time (which involves a certain amount of quantity too) with your family. You also need to have a little time to spend on yourself too. The balance is difficult at first, with all of the demands for your time, but when planned out, it works really well. For a long time, I could not figure out why I would only get 17,000 to 20,000 miles from a set of tires that were rated to give 40,000 miles. A few years ago, I leased a van. Because I was completing doctoral work at Virginia Tech, some 105 miles away from my home, I started rotating the tires and changing the oil every 2,500 to 3,000 miles. I never did this before because I thought that it would take too much time, and it would be too expensive. "After all, that's why they put those little lights in the dash...to warn you when you need to change the oil and stuff," I thought. Well, believe it or not, I didn't have to change tires until I reached 42,000 miles! This was certainly a first, and with a vehicle that was supposed to be much harder on tires than a regular passenger car, I learned two very important lessons. One, that it does not take too much time to get the tires rotated and the oil changed, and two, that it is not very costly, especially when you figure in what it "could" cost if I waited for the lights on the dash to remind me. I thought that this was also a good example for my life! I would not take time out for myself because I figured that it would take too much time, and that it would be too costly. I started to think that if I did take the time, as I did with my van, then maybe I too would get "more mileage" just like I did on that first set of tires.

Taking time out for yourself..."healthy selfish"...may well afford more miles to do more work and go more places. Without taking the time for yourself, you may have to be discarded far sooner than if you would take care of yourself!

Public Life: When we talk about public life, we address the way you act and carry out daily activities in the community where you live. What do others say about you, your ministry, etc. Sure, there will always be those who have nothing good to say about anything, and there will be people who may talk about you because you and your church are doing what they think they should be doing. But, there should also be a solid core of people who know you and believe in what you do. They have faith in you as a person, in your relationship with God, and in your interest in helping others through a care-giving ministry. Knowing your limitations in this area is important. Perhaps it shows up the most when you seek out referrals. Going to others, looking at their programs, talking with them one-on-one and understanding where they are coming from is important for developing a good referral source, but it is also important in that they may be looking for a good referral source for themselves also!

When Steven first attended the training for a care-giving ministry in his church, he was really excited. He told everyone he met what he was "being trained for," and about how much he was learning. Steven felt as though he could deal with most any situation he came up against, and was not negligent in relating his abilities to others. After the training was completed, it seemed that he wasn't being called much by the pastor or others to help. Months and months went by without his ever getting a referral to help someone. He also made it clear to anyone who would listen, and even to those who did not want to listen, about his abilities and confusion as to why a gifted man such as himself was not being used in the church. The pastor answered his questions. It was not because he was unable to help others, nor was it because he did not understand and know the materials. It was because his personal life appeared to others to be so "public" that people feared he would talk to everyone about their problems shared in confidence. They thought that whoever Dave would see would certainly be the topic to justify what a great job he had done.

Many times I conduct seminars or workshops at local businesses. I have found that people who would not usually go to a psychotherapist do call me for an appointment, not because I have told them something new and innovative, but because my public life, when I speak to their group, is one that communicates care and concern. Many people have told me that after hearing me speak and answer questions, they felt comfortable in calling for an appointment. Believe it or not, much of the success you will have in the ministry of care-giving will depend upon the type of relationship you develop with who you see. If they feel comfortable with you, your personalities seem to match, and they believe that you can help them, your sessions will go much smoother than if these qualities are not present. If you do not like the person you are counseling, discontinue seeing them. Refer them to someone who will better match their personality. Similarly, if the person you are seeing does not feel comfortable with you, they will stop coming. You as a caregiver have a lot to do with developing this warm, comfortable relationship. People who come to you will be scared and worried about their situation. It may be the very first time they have told what you will hear to anybody. It may be so personal to them that even mentioning what they need to relay is very difficult for them. If the atmosphere you create exudes safety, compassion, and strength, the task of sharing with you what is hurting them will be easier.

If you are practicing your care-giving ministry within your areas of strength, others will find out. Word gets around that you care, and that if someone needs help, you are the person to talk with. We have all heard about how bad news travels fast. Well, in the same way, good news travels also – perhaps not quite as quickly. I believe that the best referrals I get in my private practice come from patients I see in therapy. Their stamp of approval and satisfaction with the treatment I offer is better than any newspaper ad I could possibly take out. Word of mouth, personal endorsement, confidence that someone with similar problems to mine sought and got help is reassuring for the individual who is nervous and possibly distrusting of telling their story to a stranger.

Private Life: Your private life is what you hold inside, the values you adhere to, your inner commitment to self and to God. It is also what you do when no one else is around. Too many people lead double lives. They publically stand for one thing, but privately hold on to old habits or ways of thinking that are not the same. Perhaps this is what happens to people we read about who are caught in a perverse lifestyle. Or with someone, for example, who you suddenly find out has had a drinking problem for years. Still others may have some kind of sexual problem that they haven't really dealt with by turning it over to the power of God in their lives. If you have a problem area, admit this to yourself and stay far away from care-giving situations that would feed the area(s) you are battling privately. A deacon in the church, Jeff, had a drinking problem that no one else knew about. He was a caregiver, trained and looked up to by all who knew him. His frequent trips out of town seemed normal enough until he was arrested for drinking while under the influence (DUI) in a neighboring town. Deacon Jeff was ordered to therapy for a drinking problem that was far greater than even he was willing to admit. He would counsel people, in his care-giving capacity, who had drinking problems themselves, and seemed to do a good job with them. However, as Jeff later admitted, "whenever I had a person who was a drinker, I cringed inside. I knew that God was telling me that I too had this problem, that I should 'practice what I preached' to others, but I held on to my drinking. Yes, it was hard saying one thing while actively practicing the opposite, but I always figured that I would stop tomorrow. The problem was that 'tomorrow' never came on its own." In Jeff's situation, it would be unwise for him to deal with people who have a drinking problem. It would be most advisable for Jeff to first get help for his own drinking. The same principle goes for someone who harbors sexual thoughts or fantasies. It is NOT advisable for this person to counsel members of the opposite sex or couples who are having sexual problems. It IS advisable, however, for this person to ask God to help them deal with what they harbor in their mind and strive for God's cleansing. If this is not possible, it would be better for this person to resign their care-giving duties until they can be restored.

On a less dramatic level, let's suppose that you and your wife are not getting along at all. In fact, your wife is all but ready to leave you, and your children are getting into trouble at school. For you to counsel a couple who are having similar problems in their marriage would be pretty tough. Yes, the Word of God will still work in their lives, but in this example, the messenger is a potential stumbling block for God to work through. The same would be true if this person was counseling parents about their children. This does not mean the minister or others on the ministry team have to be perfect, but it does suggest that we all need to be receptive to changing our own lives, and be willing to do what needs to be done in order to meet our own family's needs as well as our individual needs. Many times, if you have gone through similar situations as the person you are helping, you can share some of how you dealt with it as an example of how God worked in your life to bring about change and healing. This self-disclosure is very helpful in showing the people you are helping that you are human too! Some patients are shocked when I tell them that I have to deal with depression at times in my life too. They say "you get depressed too?" I say, "Sure I get depressed at times. However, I have found ways that enable me to not stay depressed, and I would like to show you the techniques that have helped me."

Referral: a team effort. Another important area that interweaves between the others is knowing when and how to refer people. Referral is really a way to broaden your ministry and its effectiveness. It is a team effort that is designed to help a troubled or distressed person in need beyond what you are able to provide. A common misconception about referring someone is that it signals there is a weakness in your care-giving abilities. "If I refer this person whom I have been seeing, they as well as others, will think that I am incompetent. Confidence will be lost in my ability to counsel." I do not believe that this is true at all. Referral is not giving away responsibility! Rather, it is being honest about your abilities, strengths, and knowledge in helping the person who has come to you in need.

Proverbs 11:14 states, "Where no counsel is, the people fall: but in the multitude of counselors there is safety." I believe this means in referring, you are able to establish a larger network of safety and support that can be engaged when needed. Wayne Oates, in his book *Protestant Pastoral Counseling,* states that "One of the reasons that pastors do not have time to do their pastoral ministry is that they insist on doing it all themselves. They have failed to build a detailed knowledge of their community as to the agencies, professional and private practitioners, etc., who could help them in their task." There is no glory in being a "Lone Ranger" when other resources are available to you. Remember that even the Lone Ranger had Tonto!

If you can work through the issues of referring, and feel comfortable with it, another problem arises...when do I refer? Tom Meigs, in his article "Structured Caring," presents some guidelines for consideration in referring people you feel may need additional help:

1. People who can be helped more effectively in time, place, and training by some other person. This does not necessarily mean the person is distraught or dysfunctional. The need for help may be nothing more than a need for information or consultation.

2. People whose problems and crisis call for effective and specialized agencies within the larger community. An example of this is substance and/or alcohol abuse.

3. People whose needs are obviously beyond the caregiver's time and training.

4. People who display chronic financial needs or severe economic disability.

5. People who demonstrate a need for psychiatric care, psychotherapy, medical care, or even institutionalization.

6. People who are severely depressed or express suicidal language.

7. People who present a problem about which you know little or have limited experience.

Meigs goes on to suggest that occasionally you may get with a person about whom you have persistent negative and distractive feelings. When this happens, you may need to refer that person because your ability to listen effectively and empathetically with that person is severely prejudiced. I would add that a time to refer is also when you have very positive feelings toward a person who comes to you for help. If knowing the negative sides of their situation will in some way compromise your relationship with this person, it is better to refer.

In referring to other people or agencies, it is important that you have current, up-to-date knowledge of the resource; what they do, what type of people they see, their program, the costs involved, and how it views and works with religious people. It is also important to know and understand the type of procedures and help the person might expect to receive. Setting up a current referral file or various community and denominational resources will be very helpful early on in your development of a care-giving ministry. Personally contact and visit the various referral sources to build a personal relationship with them. This way, when you refer, they will be able to match a face with your voice. You may also find that these referral sources, when they have someone who is looking for a church to attend, will "refer" to you!

CHAPTER FIVE

CHAPTER FIVE
Confidentiality

One of my favorite verses in the Old Testament is found in the book of Proverbs. This book has so many timely sayings and ideas that are appropriate for everyday life. A favorite verse of mine is found in Chapter 25, verse 19, which states: "Confidence in an unfaithful man in time of trouble is like a broken tooth, and a foot out of joint."

This verse has always intrigued me because of the completeness of what it says in so few words. If we place our confidence in someone who is not faithful to being able to or wanting to help us when we need it, we are in serious trouble. When this happens, we are hampered in not only what we say (broken tooth idea), but also in where we go (foot out of joint idea)...and both of these are very painful!

I do not know if you have had the "wonderful" experience of having root canal work done in your mouth. Or maybe you have bitten into something that was harder than you thought, which resulted in your breaking a tooth off. Either experience is a terrific way to lose weight, but is also very painful. You cannot eat because of the pain, it is difficult to talk because of the pain, and many times the pain is so intense that your sleep is adversely affected. For those of you who can identify with this type of pain, let's go one step further. Let's say that along with the mouth pain, you have also disjointed your foot. Now, not only is it difficult to talk, eat, and maybe sleep, it is almost impossible for you to walk around too! Think of it. Not being able to eat, sleep, walk, and having a hard time explaining any of it to someone else because of the pain in your mouth. This is truly the picture of a miserable individual. It is certainly a place that I would never want to find myself in.

But, how many people do we put in that very same position when we do not hold what is told to us in private, in the strictest of confidence; when what is told to the pastor in confidence gets "preached" at the next Sunday sermon. Or when someone has for the first time told their deepest secrets to someone that they trusted to help them, and similar information is haphazardly mentioned in a social gathering or to someone who felt a need to tell others "so that they could pray for the individual."

Being a caregiver holds a great responsibility to keeping our mouths shut with information told to us in confidence. A few exceptions should be pointed out to all people you see before they share information with you. These two exceptions are valid for you to hold to because they can cause you, the caregiver, great legal and ethical trouble.

1. When a person tells you that they have either physically or sexually abused a child, most state laws require you to report this information to a local social services person. If a person tells me that they have been abusing a child, I try to have them call the department of social services with me present. I have no problems with helping someone who wants help and is willing to take the first step in getting that help. But, I am not willing to go to jail for someone who is doing wrong because I don't want to say anything. It is not your option to stick your head in the sand once you know of an abusive situation. Most state laws require you to protect the welfare of children, which involves taking the necessary steps in reporting such crimes to the proper authorities. If you believe that you can say nothing, and it is found out that you did in fact know of abuse going on, you may be on your way to jail!

2. You cannot pledge complete confidentiality if the person you are seeing tells you that they plan to kill

themself or if they plan to harm someone else. If they are suicidal, you need to take appropriate actions that will insure their safety (see Chap. 9 about crisis counseling). If they plan to harm someone else, it is your responsibility to inform the other person that they are in danger. Think of what would happen if you saw someone for the first time and they were really upset. They told you that it was entirely another person's fault and that as soon as they left your office, they were going to teach them a lesson. There was no doubt in your mind that this person was determined to and able to inflict harm. You believed that the next time this person saw the object of their hate and bitterness, that someone would either be dead or in the hospital. Let's say that you knew this other person. You don't want to get involved, so when the person leaves your office, you pray for the situation, but do nothing to warn the other person. You "leave it in God's hands," and go about your daily tasks. Sure it seemed very important, and you were very concerned. You prayed, and prayed a lot, but did nothing to warn the other person. You almost forget about it when the telephone awakens you at 2:30 in the morning. On the other end of the line is a woman who is very upset, crying, and calling you from the local emergency room. She relays that her husband was severely beaten up and stabbed by a man and the doctors are not sure if he will live or not.

I don't know about you, but I shudder to think of something like that happening to me. "Maybe it would not have happened if only I had called this person to tell them that someone had told me that they meant to do them harm. Maybe I would not have been awakened in the early morning, had to go to the hospital, or worse yet, had to go to the funeral home if only I would have let them know when I should have."

Confidentiality relates to what we say and who we say it to. It also refers to who has access to our notes, files, and documents. For anyone else to have access, other than the caregiver, is inviting trouble. It is all right for other care-giving team members (including the pastor) to know where they are in case you are unavailable and there is a need to know what's been done, but to allow secretaries, associates, etc., to have access to these private notes is definitely a no-no. I suggest not having secretaries type your notes. It seems to me that by having a secretary type the information obtained in your sessions, you are placing thoughts, feelings, and information on them that may overburdening. Even if the person is the most tight-lipped person ever created by God, sometimes the information contained in your private notes can be more than someone else needs to deal with emotionally.

In starting a care-giving ministry, check with other pastors, and professionals (Licensed Professional Counselors, Social Workers) to find out what your particular state requires of you. Knowing what your obligations are and what boundaries, with respect to confidentiality, you should operate within is very important. Knowing these guidelines will also serve as a baseline protocol for what to do should an emergency situation arise. Each member of your care-giving team will need to know exactly what to do so that their actions will do the most good for the person they are seeing while not putting your ministry in jeopardy. It will also protect them from legal considerations should a situation arise that comes to the attention of the court system.

Checking with area professionals will also help you establish guidelines for what you can share and with whom you can share it. For example, suppose that you are seeing a 17-year-old. His father calls you after you have seen this young man 3 or 4 times, and wants you to tell him everything his son has told you. What do you do? Is it a breach of confidentiality to share all? If you do so, what about the trust developed between you and this young man? If you do not, what steps can the father legally take?

I have had situations where a mother called, wanting to know what was going on with her married daughter, and when her next appointment was. My response to this very angry woman was, "If you want information about your daughter, I would suggest that you take that up with her." Her response was that she was going to have her attorney talk to me, so I readily gave her my phone number along with the correct spelling of my name. A good rule of thumb, when talking with a minor, is to talk with them about "what if?" In other words, ask them, "What if...your parents call and want me to tell them what's going on. What do you want me to do?" You can think up other scenarios that would cover what they wish you to do. However, it is helpful if you already know what your legal responsibilities are before getting into one of these situations. Look up phone numbers in your local phone book for professionals you can talk to, if you do not know of someone in your church. Ask them questions that cover different situations of confidentiality and be sure that you understand what to do, why you are doing it, and what happens if you do not comply.

CHAPTER SIX

CHAPTER SIX
Do's and Don'ts of Care-giving

When a person comes to you for counseling, it is easy to forget all of the things that you told yourself you would remember. Many times, when the person leaves your office that little voice rattles in your head asking you if you asked this or that; if you did this or said that correctly, etc. Below is a list of common *Do's* and *Don'ts* to remember in the care-giving session. The more you see people in counseling, the easier you will be able to assimilate these into your normal approach to care-giving. Until then, however, here are some reminders:

Do's

1. Set the individual at ease. This is done when you first greet the individual coming to see you for the first time. It also applies to people you see in your everyday life, but for the first time in a care-giving context. Decorate your reception area and office in such a manner that comfortable and secure feelings are exuded. Earth-tone colors contribute to this atmosphere, along with having enough seating space and appropriate reading materials.

If you have a secretary, he or she will be a prime person for verbally setting the atmosphere. A friendly smile, warm words of encouragement, direction and clarification for filling out intake forms, and so forth, are helpful. If coffee is available, this person could offer some to the people you are about to see. They can then let the people know that you will be informed that they are here and are filling out the forms.

If you do not have a full-time secretary, you yourself can greet the people with a smile and warm handshake. Give them an intake form to fill out, along with whatever directions they may need. Offer them some coffee.

Let them know that they can fill out the forms in the waiting room and that you will return shortly to get started.

2. Ask discerning questions. Once counselees enter your office, direct them to where they are to sit. You may begin the session by looking over their intake form, and asking, "How can I be of help to you today?" Allow them to put into words, the reason they have come to see you. Many times it is helpful to boil down their statements into manageable sentences by rephrasing what has been said. This allows the reason(s) for their seeing you to become more clear, and communicates that you understand what they are looking for in counseling. If what they say is unclear to you, ask, "Do you mean that you are looking for..." or "Am I correct in thinking that you are asking that they..."

Usually it is better to phrase your questions in a way that cannot be answered with a simple "yes" or "no" answer. One way to accomplish this is to ask "What" questions rather than "Why" questions. For example, rather than asking "Why did you say that to her?" you may choose to ask "What brought you to the point that you needed to question her in that way?" or, instead of saying "Why were you late?" you could ask "What was going on that caused you to arrive late?" Using a "What" question tends to illicit a more full-bodied response from the person, and goes further in helping you understand what was going on and how you can help. In addition, asking a "What" question tends to evoke a reason for their action, whereas a "Why" question tends to illicit more of an excuse for their actions.

Another important thing to remember here is that many times, it is more important to "see" what the person is saying than it is to "hear" what they are saying. What I mean by this is that people communicate not only with the words they speak, but also with their body movements and posture. If a person says verbally that they are comfortable and open to discuss something, yet their arms are folded around their chest, they are sitting on the edge of the chair, and appear to nervously be looking around the room a lot, they are non-verbally saying something quite different. It would be a mistake to listen with your ears and operate on what you heard as fact, while disqualifying the behavior you see before you. You may say to yourself, "What I heard doesn't match with what I am seeing. I wonder why they seem to be so uptight even though they said that they were comfortable and open to talk. Maybe I should address what I see, their uncomfortableness and defensiveness, before we get into this subject."

3. Focus on specific problems. Many times when people come in for counseling, they tend to combine a lot of problems into one big one. Some of the ingredients for the "really BIG" problem with which they need help comes from the past, and sometimes they are borrowed from the future. "My husband is always late. He was late for our first date 18 years ago, and he'll be late for his own funeral." It is important to focus on whether or not his being late is contributing to their present situation or not. At times, statements like this are said to "appraise" the counselor of the pervasiveness of being late but has little to do with the current topic for which they seek counseling.

Another common problem is for people to "glob" a lot of little problems together until they get so big that life itself seems overwhelming. A technique you can use is to tell them that dealing with problems is like eating a pizza. Go on to explain that when you go to a pizzeria very hungry, you feel like you could eat the entire pizza in one bite. However, the pizza shop helps you with this decision by cutting the pizza into slices. No matter how hungry you are, you eat one slice at a time, one bite at a time until your slice is eaten. Then you go to the next slice and repeat the same procedure – bite, chew, swallow; bite, chew, swallow; and so on until the second piece is finished. You repeat this same mechanism until you have satisfied your hunger or until the available slices are gone.

In the same way, people can learn to deal with their problems – one at a time. The problems have to be specifically identified (much like ordering specific toppings on your pizza), and the big mass of "globbed" together problems must be divided – much like the individual slices of your pizza. Then, one at a time, the counselee is instructed to take specific steps in dealing with each problem until it is "finished off," much like you would eat each slice of pizza. The value of using an example such as this is that it can be reinforced over and over, day in and day out by the person every time they eat. Each meal, and each bite, chew, swallow will reinforce the process they need to maintain to successfully deal with problems as they come up, rather than letting them "glob" together until they become overbearing.

4. Get them to face reality as soon as possible. When people come to you with marital problems, sometimes one (or both) deny the significance of their situation. This is especially true when severe marital discord has gone to the point that one of the persons wants out of the relationship, or when there has been infidelity in the relationship. The person who wants to stay in the relationship or the one who has not had the affair many times denies the reality of what their partner wants to or has done. If this person continues to "fantasize" the reality of their situation, you may need to help them focus and face the stark reality of the problem at hand. Another situation when this is evident is when a loved one dies and the survivor must continue on. Helping the survivors face the reality that the loved one has passed away, and assisting them in the process of living is very difficult because it can be a hard reality for some to face.

5. Get them to focus on present attitudinal/behavioral problems. People easily bring up the past. Sometimes this is such a problem that it may appear that they must live in the past because it is so clear to them. Things that happened 5, 7, 10+ years ago seem to have happened only yesterday. Past hurts, bitterness for things said or done, things that "could have" been done or said, along with things that shouldn't have been done or said are very current and invade the present situation for which they are seeking help.

It is important to have people focus on their present situation. Remind them that the only thing about the past they can change is the way they look at it. It is true that we, many times, have hurtful and terrible things happen to us. However, it is important to remind counselees that we are responsible for how we deal with whatever God allows to come into our lives. We are unable to control others, what they do or say, and we are usually unable to control our environment in such a way as to always work for us. But, we are able to develop a reliance upon God that He is in control of everything that happens to us, and because of this belief in a plan for our life, that whatever happens is for a reason.

The focus needs to shift from the past (or future only) to the present. "Are you allowing God to teach you through all that is taking place in your life?" "What does God want you to learn from this situation?" "What do you need to do?" and "How do you need to think differently to be successful in this situation?" are some questions to ask.

6. Identify specific changes that need to be made. Someone has said that if you pray in general, your prayers will be answered in general; but if you pray specifically, your prayers will be answered specifically. This is the same rationale when identifying what the problems are, and in developing a plan to deal with them. If the person you are seeing says, "Well, I guess that I need to be more loving to my partner," they are probably talking about their needing to do more of the same behaviors toward their mate that haven't worked yet. This is not what needs to be done. Rather, your task is to assist them in looking at *specific* changes that need to be made in relating to their mate, and identify what needs to change along with exactly how that change will look. If you allow a person to make changes in their behavior (or thinking) in general terms, both of you will be disappointed. If, on the other hand, you identify specific areas that need to be changed, along with helping them look at exactly what needs to be done to show that real change has taken place, you are well on the way to being successful.

7. *Try to bring them to a commitment to change.* Once you have assisted the person in identifying what needs to happen for change to occur, it is important to have them commit to change. When a person tells me, "Well, I'll try," I usually respond with something like, "I'm not sure what you mean by saying I'll try." This usually baffles the person who cannot believe that you are so ignorant as to not understand what they are saying. This also opens their (mental) doors to hear what you mean.

When a person says, "I'll try," they could mean one of several things. Does it mean that they will "think" about doing the assignment? Will they fulfill (only) a portion of what they say they will do and decide it is too much work to finish the assignment? Or will they have all good intentions to do the assignment but just get too busy and forget until the night before coming to see you and in their haste, quickly write or do "something" that can only be viewed as half-hearted? As you can see with these few examples, there are a lot of reasons for saying that you don't know what they mean when they tell you "I'll try."

It is best to explain your confusion, allow them to think you a fool, and explain why you are confused. Most of the time, they will understand more fully your confusion, and your I.Q. will have raised a considerable amount in their estimation. They will also have to deal with the question of whether they will actually DO the homework assignment or not...clearly and simply.

8. Give them a simple step-by-step plan to change. This doesn't have to be a long, drawn-out process. If you have in mind the pizza metaphor (in # 3), it is easier to assist people in identifying changes that need to be made, and the sequence by which they should proceed. Allow the person to be the main contributor in the development of a game plan. Assist them in clearly identifying the proper sequence of steps that need to be taken to ensure success. Remember that God plans everything in its own time. Nothing happens out of sequence from its appointed time and all is done decently and in an orderly fashion. This is the format to encourage the person you are seeing to follow. Do specific things in the right time and in an orderly way.

If you do not have a clear, concrete understanding of exactly what the problems are, it will be impossible to help construct a viable plan to effectively deal with the situation. If you have some concerns as to specifically what the problem is, now is the time to redefine it. Maybe this is mostly for your benefit, but it will ensure that you have all the facts available to you before developing a game plan.

9. Develop an atmosphere of hope in the session. While people will come to see you for a number of reasons, one of the common threads that bond them all together is their need for hope. They need to know that there is hope for them in their particular situation. When problems get too big for us to handle, it is easy to lose hope. Hope that things will get better often turns to

despair that they never will. Your part in this is to encourage the people in need of help that God has allowed
you to counsel as a caregiver. Encourage them that
there is hope. And that this hope is for them – in their
situation, and with the guidance of the Holy Spirit, you
will assist them in finding the answers needed for them
to be successful.

The atmosphere of hope extends beyond what you
say, into how you act. If you are gloomy and negative, it
will be very difficult to encourage anyone no matter
what you say to them. If, on the other hand, you exemplify a hopefulness in helping others with difficulties
that springs from a personal life that has weathered
hardship, and exude a hope that has faced the fires of
discouragement, despair and hopelessness, your demeanor will go far in creating an atmosphere of hope to
others.

*10. Get them to identify their own progress in
evaluating the problem.* There is no value in creating
a dependency on you for the counselee. Ultimately, your
care-giving sessions need to be a laboratory where they
find answers, test hypothesis, and learn to "walk on
their own" again. When faced with a similar situation in
their life, the counselee should be encouraged and
taught how to evaluate the situation and know how to
progress through to a successful conclusion. It is fine if
they need assistance from you or another during this
time, but they should be encouraged to confront themselves and do more on their own. If you do not teach
them how to deal with similar situations, you will create
an emotional cripple who is unable to face the chal-
lenges of life and the opportunities of God that are,
many times, forged through adversity. When first learning how to ride a two-wheel bicycle, many of us used
training wheels. This devise was secured to either side
of the rear wheel to ensure that we would not fall should
our balance become compromised. As balance developed,

the training wheels were removed and, though a little wobbly at times, we were able to maneuver the two-wheeled bicycle without the assistance of the training wheels.

How silly it would look for an adult to ride a bike with training wheels. And how discouraging it would be to have a person you have helped depend upon you throughout life instead of learning to balance their life upon the steady hand of God. Through any situation we face, God is there to keep us balanced. Sometimes He sends godly men and women to assist us, but through it all, He wants us to learn how to steady our minds and thoughts upon Him. He is the one that we must turn people toward to depend on. We as His servants are used at times to clarify and discern truths to others, and the counseling session is a time for this. We are not to gather people around us who depend solely upon us because of our relationship with God; rather, we are to encourage them to strengthen their relationship with God, and "prove" Him to be all that He wants to be in their lives.

As with a coin, there are always two sides to a subject. This is also the case when it comes to the do's and don'ts in counseling. You have already looked over the do's, but there are also some don'ts involved in this process. Remember that these are things you want the counselee to avoid doing. By your understanding what they are, and staying abreast of them in the care-giving session, you will enable the person to use the time spent in with you to better understand themselves, their situation, and how God plays an important role in the outcome. Below are a list of don'ts along with a brief explanation of each. This list, as the previous one, is not meant to be exhaustive. Rather they serve as highlights for you to remember.

Don'ts

1. Don't allow the person to act completely on their feelings. It is true that we all have feelings and emotions. Without them, life would be boring to say the least. However, while feelings are an important part of life, they are not designed to be the sole foundation by which we make decisions. For some, feelings are the basis for experiencing life. Popular statements have characterized this emphasis with phrases like, "If it feels good, do it," and "How could it be so wrong when it feels so right?" Many people get so wound up in their feelings that their good sense gets lost in the shuffle. Only after the fact do they many times say, "Gee, I wish I would have thought that through a little more!"

People you see will have a tremendous amount of feelings whirling around because of the situation for which they come to see you. Helping the person feel comfortable *(Do's #1)* and guiding them to focus on the specifics of their situation *(Do's #3)* will help them put their feelings about the situation in their proper place. Recognize the emotion that is generated from their turmoil. Don't discount their emotions as something that is merely getting in the way. Rather, say to the person something along the line of: "I can see that this really upsets you, and that emotions are running high right now. What we need to do with the time we have together is to focus on what you need to do when you leave my office, until we get together again at our next session."

This type of statement lets the counselee know that you understand their emotions are strong, yet do not discount them as an irritable fact of life. Gently direct the focus on what needs to be done in the time constraints that your session allows. It also suggests that you are there to assist in developing of a plan that they can implement today and carry through until you meet again.

2. *Don't allow the person to avoid problems.* If the person needs to deal with certain problems, help them do so. Many times these problems surround confronting someone about what was said. Other times, the issue at hand involves what another person has done or not done. In the healing process of the counseling experience, it is important to guide the counselee in confronting others that have contributed to the difficulties they are facing.

It is also important to keep in mind that confrontation deals not only with others, but many times focuses internally to what the person is doing, saying or thinking. Self-confrontation is the first place to start, because many problems exist because people are not willing to look at themselves first. When David was chased by his son Absolom, he cried unto God in despair because his own son wanted to kill him. David prayed to God to "Search me, O God, and know my heart..." (Ps. 139:23). It seems that David knew he had to be a clean vessel before he could ask God to deal with the other troubling circumstances in his life that were out of his direct control.

3. *Don't allow the person to blame others.* The easiest thing for people to do is to point the finger of blame to others. Sometimes, the finger is pointed at "anyone" else, so long as it is not pointed back to the one pointing. The interesting fact is that as we physically point a finger toward someone else, we have three fingers pointing back toward us! When you actually point this out to the counselee, by holding up your hand and pointing, the visual realization of this gesture becomes a reality for them.

Encourage people you see to examine their lives, their motives, and their thoughts before casting blame and anger onto others. As I have said, this is a very hard thing for most people to do. It is not a self-righteous exercise, nor is it a "I'm the victim" game. Rather, it is the starting point for having God work in the person's life in a way that perhaps He hasn't been allowed to before. A new beginning, a stronger faith, and a clearer view as to God's purpose in allowing the situation for which you are meeting, may be found.

4. Don't allow the person to lose hope. Many people who seek help from you have lost hope. They have lost hope in dealing successfully with their situation, they have lost hope in their ability to solve their problem, and they have lost hope in God intervening on their behalf. As mentioned in the Do's list #9, you are a visual representation of hope. People who come to you for counseling are in need of hope. You as a man or woman of God are an instrument, a visual representation of hope for them. The atmosphere you create is important, but the realness of your person, along with how you conduct yourself – in a godly and knowledgeable way – is by far the greater example of hope.

5. Don't allow the person to remain undisciplined and disorganized. Chances are that part of the reason a person has come to you is that some area of their life is undisciplined and disorganized. It may be that their thought life is undisciplined or their actions have become undisciplined to the point that another person is involved in their life. On the other hand, it may also be true that they have allowed so many things to pile up on them that they are very disorganized in their normal routines. Large amounts of stress or crisis situations can cause a person to become disorganized in their normally organized routines.

Assist the person in sorting out the situations that are causing them to flounder in their disorganization and undisciplined lifestyle. Look at each facet of their situation, and help them to straighten the crooked lines of their thought and actions. Take one step at a time, in a practical step-by-step program that they understand, agree with, and can follow. Make sure that the steps taken can be recognized as being completed when they are finished.

6. Don't allow the person to stop without forgiveness. Forgiveness is very important to the healing process. It needs to be applied not only to the offending parties, but also to self. Forgiving self is many times a very hard thing for people to do. It is often overlooked as a necessary area for forgiveness to be applied. However, if we do not forgive ourselves, how will we be able to forgive others?

Sometimes people get stuck with the concept of forgiveness. They will often say: "They hurt me so bad that they don't deserve to be forgiven." Often, this is true. However, the concept of forgiveness is not based upon the merits of the offending party "earning" it. Rather, it is a "healthy-selfish" concept. Maybe the other person doesn't deserve to be forgiven but you deserve (and are encouraged in Scripture) to forgive. When we forgive others even though they do not merit it, we free ourselves from the burden of remembering the offense, which allows the healing process to begin within us. It is a concept that we need. We deserve the freedom that forgiveness has to offer.

Once a person has accepted the concept of forgiveness for themselves, it is important for them to act like it. People tend to forgive others, but this is an inward application that many times loses its effectiveness because it is not demonstrated outside of self. Stress to the person you are counseling that they need to consider acting like they have forgiven themselves, and/or others. Show outwardly what you have covenanted in your heart and mind before God. Don't forgive just to make yourself or others who know about the situation, feel better, do something about it!

7. Don't allow the person to talk about another person behind their back. This most commonly happens when you see a husband or wife without their spouse being present. All to often, it is the wife who first enters counseling because of problems in her relationship. Make it a point to not allow her to talk about her husband when he is not present. There are a number of reasons for this stand. One, the other person is not there to defend themselves. If you allow her to continually talk about him (and they usually are not admonishing the high points of his personality), you run the risk of becoming biased in your thinking towards him. It is very hard to disallow what is being said by the counselee when they were one of the people who lived through the situation. Again, as with the coin, each story has two sides!

If your intent is to get the husband into the caregiving process, it is important that you eliminate as many road blocks to his hesitation as possible. I believe that there are two main reasons why a husband would not enter counseling. One is because he simply does not want to enter into anything that would prolong the relationship. In other words, he isn't interested in making the marriage work. Through your questioning, you will be able to ascertain whether or not this is the situation. If they are still living together and doing some things together, this is not usually the case. The second reason a husband will not join your sessions is because he may feel that he has been talked about so much by his wife to you that he won't have a fair chance. He already argues with his wife, so why would he want to talk to someone who has been filled with information given by his partner too!

An important boundary to set early in the first session is that you do not want to talk about someone who isn't there. This is different than relating the absent person's involvement in the situation. Frequently at the end of the first or second counseling session, the wife is wanting for the husband to come for the next session. It is wise to tell her to relay to her husband that, "The counselor told me that he would not talk about someone behind their back. So, we talked about me. He told me that it would not be fair to talk about you when you were not here to share your side, so we didn't." If the husband is interested in the relationship, the barrier or having the cards already stacked against him will be removed. Your task is to make sure that you honor what you have told them!

8. Don't allow the person to give up when they fail. People tend to view only success as something that they can learn from. They often believe that when they succeed God has blessed them and answered the fervent prayers of their heart. However, it would appear that the greater lessons learned from God are those forged through the fires of adversity and failure. Sometimes people fail because they haven't learned that they are to go about it in a different way. Other times, they fail because it is more of an "I want" than a "God wants for me" attitude. Still other situations fail because it is not the right timing for success to happen. Whatever the reason (and I am sure there are many more of them), show the person that failure is only a response to what they have tried. It does not mean that they should give up; it does not mean that they are a failure; nor does it mean that God does not want them to be successful. Rather, it means that there is something to learn from what and how they tried to deal with the situation.

An old saying says, "If at first you don't succeed, try, try again." I can only partially agree with this one. I do agree that if you don't succeed the first time, you should try again and again. I do not agree, however with the implication that you should try and try in the same old way! It seems to me that if you try the same-ol', same-ol', then the same-ol' thing will happen – NOTHING! Instead, I believe that if you try one way and it doesn't work out, you should look to see why it didn't work. Then, try again with the information gained from the first try. The process of learning from failures is the true secret of a successful person. Remember examples of saints praying over and over for God to answer; the setbacks of men and women of God, and the strength and insight they gained from these failures. Sometimes, the way we learn is from our mistakes. If you don't make mistakes, you don't learn!

9. Don't allow the person to generalize rather than specify. This has to do mainly with the information they share in the care-giving session. It is easy for people to not only generalize what the problems are in their lives, but to also speak in general when they discuss their involvement in the present situation. Strive to ask specific questions that cannot be answered with a simple "Yes" or "No" response. When we pray, it is better to pray specifically, rather than generally.

When talking to a couple, I will ask them both to list seven things they can do to show their partner that they love them. Many times the lists come back with very general terms listed. For example, if one writes: "Be more loving," I get very confused as to what that means. I am further lost when trying to understand how being more loving could be demonstrated in such a way that the person recognizes it. Anyone reading this right now, has their own interpretation of how to be more loving. But for the husband and wife sitting in your office, this is not what is wanted or desired. Who cares what someone else's opinion is about how to fulfill your request for being more loving? What is important to the person requesting this is that they see the actions of their mate as actually producing the fulfillment of "being more loving."

Unless you keep the people you see in specific, concrete images, all of you will be very frustrated. Ask the person making the request; "Exactly what do you mean by *being more loving?*" Have them list specifically what they are looking for, so that when their mate does these things, it will be taken as being "more loving."

10. Do not allow the person to become dependent upon you. This is perhaps one of the most important things for you to keep in mind. The person can easily become dependent upon you because of the atmosphere of acceptance, your taking the time to listen and understand, along with your giving hope and encouragement. This does not serve a good purpose. The only purpose it could fill is the stroking of your ego. If this is the case, you should not read any further, rather you should put this book down, and resign your position as a caregiver.

If this is not your situation, keep on constant guard for the person you are seeing to develop a dependence toward you. Some signs that this may be developing or has already happened are:

* If the person always has to talk to you before doing something.

* You sense that the person needs your approval before doing something.

* The person is calling you more than usual "just to talk."

* The person sets up numerous appointments to see you, without a crisis.

* The person continues to balk at completing assignments you give them.

* If you sense that the person is getting more "personal" needs met from your sessions together than they are help for a particular situation.

* If the person tries to extend the session past the time needed to deal with their particular situation.

CHAPTER SEVEN

CHAPTER SEVEN
Counseling Family Strife

Marriage and family are social institutions which our society both praises and derides. These two institutions provide the opportunity for the most intimate of human relationships and can bring either meaningful fulfillment or despairing agony.

Marriage is one in the series of life's phases, each one presenting its own particular adjustment and unique problems. During adolescence, we face the development of a stable self-identity and the determination of our role in life. Marriage presents the problem of learning to achieve true personal intimacy. If the adolescent's quest of becoming a self-reliant person has not been achieved, a young couple may find it difficult to learn the importance of being an individual and being a couple in the process of sharing with each other. Too many times couples I see in treatment believe that they have to give up being a person because they are married. These people, over the years, become more and more bitter because their identity is solely wrapped up in being "Bob's wife," or "Jennifer's husband," or "Billy and Joe's mother or father." Lack of identity as an individual leads to enmeshment and frustration.

There's nothing wrong with having an "individual" identity and a "couples" identity at the same time, as long as the expression of either does not violate the functioning of the other. In other words, it is fine for Jennifer to be known to others as Jennifer. Not just as Bob's wife, or Billy and Joe's mother. True, she is Bob's wife, and she is Billy and Joe's mother, but she is also Jennifer the person! She will probably have some interests and maybe even enjoy activities that Bob does not. Her involvement in these does not mean that she is not interested in and working (as Bob is) toward a close intimate relationship with her husband. Rather, it means that she is an individual with individual tastes and talents. She is able to express these in a way that is glorifying to God, and in a way that does not take time away from being a couple and a family. If being and expressing yourself as an individual violates the time and energy needed to be an intimate couple, then there is a problem. Likewise, if being a couple strangles either person to the point that they cannot be an individual, a serious look at what is going on is strongly suggested.

This is what I like to call Phase I, achieving intimacy-oneness. As God's Word tells us, "they two shall be one flesh" (Eph. 5:31). Notice that this idea of oneness is a process that two people embark upon when they marry. It is the process of going through other phases that make up the marital relationship. These phases are as follows:

Phase I – The early years.

Phase II – Pregnancy and childhood.

Phase III – Mid-life; children in school.

Phase IV – Late adulthood; children leave home; parenting parents.

Phase V – Retirement and aging.

Phase VI – Single again; death of spouse.

Keep in mind that this outline of marriage is not perfect. Death, separation, and divorce can create a disruption in these phases. These, along with other situations that happen in life, are also opportunities for ministry to the caregiver.

When you are a caregiver and begin to see an individual or couple, remember that each family is unique in its own system of communication. If early in marriage, a husband and wife do not learn to communicate clearly to each other in both word and actions, they are very likely to have great difficulty in their marriage. This also hampers their effectiveness in praying!

One of the concepts that you need to keep in mind, when talking with a couple who are believers, is that there are three vital elements of communication. When these three (human) elements are functioning well in a relationship, a couple can usually go through almost anything that comes their way. It should be understood that a foundation for any marriage is a personal commitment to Christ as Lord and Savior and with this foundational commitment (salvation) working in their lives, not only can they be successful in dealing with most any situation, they can become closer to each other (the process of becoming one) as a result!

These three elements are:

1. Good communication.

2. Effective listening.

3. The willingness to negotiate (or personally change).

Good communication is different from "talking." It is giving and receiving information. Hearing what the other person says, both verbally and behaviorally, is important. Of the three ways we communicate – verbally, behaviorally, and tone inflections – the most listened to form of communication is behavioral. Behavioral means our actions. For years, people have understood that the most effective way to communicate is through your actions. "Talk is cheap," "Practice what you preach," "Walk your talk," and "Don't tell me, show me," are but a few phrases that come to mind when talking about communication. When our words do not match what we do, people usually tend to believe what they see rather than what they hear.

Effective listening is an active process. It involves allowing the other person time to say what they need to say. It also includes your attentiveness to what they are saying. If you do not understand what they are saying, it's OK to either restate what you thought you heard, or ask them to clarify what was said. Many times people jump in with their comments as soon as the other person pauses to take a breath of air. They weren't finished talking, they just needed air! But, with this ever so small gap of silence, the other person jumps in with their (usually) long-winded comments. The message the person gets is "you didn't hear anything I was saying. You did not even let me finish what I was saying!"

A willingness to negotiate is vital to this process. If two people, with different opinions, communicate and listen effectively to each other, then the necessity to change is evident and obvious. Because there is a conflict, there is also the need to change. Communication that is clear, direct, understood and heard accurately, will tend to lift the fogginess of confusion and allow a clearer path of change to be seen. Being able to communicate well provides the road map for change. They will be able to "communicate" about what needs to be done, what each needs to do, and what result they both need to see.

This is a great opportunity for you, as a caregiver, to help guide the family in learning to communicate. The ability to openly and fully express one's ideas and feelings to one's spouse and children is perhaps crucial to resolving family tensions. It may well prove to be the KEY to restoring the family itself!

"OK, so how do I help this couple I am counseling start to communicate effectively?" Well, I'm glad that you asked! One of the best things to do is to first listen and understand what is going on. If you start right out with a few verses, you may quote and try to apply principles that do not really have a bearing on their situation. Once you have an understanding of what's going on, it is appropriate to share Scripture. Scripture is powerful. It declares that marriage is a commitment to each other for life. If their relationship is to be healthy, and for life, there must be a different type of communication than what has been going on up to this point. To have a different type of communication necessitates that certain changes be made. Follow the guidelines as mentioned earlier in this chapter, and even share with the couple the three elements of communication.

One of my favorite ways to open up communication with a family is a technique called "Table-Talk." No, tables do not talk, people do. But, tables do listen! Ask all family members to draw a sketch of the table where they sit together to eat most of their meals at home. Then, place each family member in their respective place.

Examples:

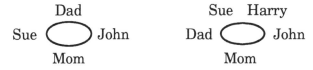

Then, ask all family members to draw a line to the one person that they talk with the most. Here is where our listening skills will be called into play.

Ask the question, "Why do you talk most with Mom and leave Dad and/or Brother out of the conversation?" Listen carefully, always remaining neutral. Sometimes members of families will form alliances with other family members. Do not get caught in a triangularization of two family members and you "against" another family member. Avoid being manipulated or maneuvered. Do not let people pull you over to their side...remain NEUTRAL!

Then, help the family define the situation and a correct perspective as to what the real issues are that have brought you all together. This leaves three very clear steps you may choose to put into practice:

1. Pinpoint the problem. Many times is isn't "the other person" ONLY!
2. Seek alternatives and solutions.
3. Help the family establish goals to deal with the problem at hand.

Remember the three action words:

1. *Pinpoint*
2. *Seek*
3. *Help*

Marriage and family problems affect us all. Ask questions if you do not understand something. Strive to make it very clear that this process is a "team-effort." Marriage and family problems are among the most commonly brought subjects to the professional counselor and the pastor. Your role will be to help facilitate change and give insight into their problematic situation. Often we, and especially the pastor, face some dilemmas. Some of them are:

1. Usually we know all (or many) of the family members before us.

2. You must always be alert to your having a bias just because you know one of the family members.

3. Be alert to tensions and changes in your own marriage and family situation.

4. Do not be afraid to offer guidance in selecting a Licensed Professional Counselor or family agency when the subject matter is outside your area of expertise and training.

5. Always communicate the truth of the Scriptures as it relates to families.

One of the most enjoyable times with a married couple is to present a Bible study of a passage relating to family, the covenant of marriage, the empty-nest syndrome, etc. I believe that your role as a caregiver will bring great satisfaction and a joy that goes beyond understanding, to your life.

A few years ago, pastor Bob was involved with a young newlywed couple. They were about to call it quits, according to the husband. "All she ever does is complain," the husband blurted. "She knew when we first married that I hunted, fished, and played ball. What does she want me to do? Does she expect for me to stop doing these things just because of a wedding ring?" Pastor Bob began their first session with prayer and listened intently. He also watched their facial expressions and body movements. As is always the case, the husband's story had another side to it so pastor Bob asked the young wife how she saw their situation. "I feel so alone when my husband is gone," she lamented. "Rather than stay in the house all alone, I usually ride over to see Mom and Dad. When he comes back and I'm over at my parent's house, our fights begin. He doesn't think that I should spend time at my parent's house and should be there whenever he gets home."

After hearing "opening comments" from each person, pastor Bob suggested some possible options for each. He turned to the Word of God for direction and guidance. "Ephesians 5: 19-33 gives us a look at God's plan for a family." He explained that the goal is for two people who are as opposite as night and day to grow and develop together so that they actually become one. He used the example of a railroad train track. "Even though from where you are standing in the middle of a railroad track, the tracks are spread far apart, as you look into the distance they appear to merge down the line. This is an idea of what the passage in Ephesians means. The two of you can be very hardened in your expectations of yourself and each other but as you seek God's direction, communicate with Him and each other, your views and thoughts come together and merge together."

Pastor Bob explained further that verse 21 seems to set the tenor for the implementation of becoming one in Christ. "Submitting yourselves one to another" is the key, he told them. He went on to further explain how this could be done in their situation, citing practical ways and examples for both husband and wife. After a few times of meeting together, much prayer and the teaching of God's Word, they began to experience what seemed to be a renewal in their marriage. Once again, God's Word proved to be the perfect "prescription" for this troubled marriage, and for this young Christian couple. Two years later, God blessed them with the birth of their first child. As pastor Bob left the hospital maternity ward, he thought to himself, "Yes I walked down a long rocky road with this couple and God rewarded our prayer and commitment to helping them become closer to God and each other. These two people are truly learning to become one and God has blessed them with the child they wanted."

This couple had learned (and are continuing) to share and communicate with God and each other more effectively than ever before. The victory this couple experienced was foundational to their starting a strong Christian family and to their personal fulfillment. It was also a tremendous blessing to pastor Bob who was God's instrument for change. What a tremendous opportunity for a ministry that God has given to His people.

CHAPTER EIGHT

CHAPTER EIGHT
Counseling Grief

The dictionary defines "grief" as "intense emotional suffering caused by loss, disaster, misfortune, etc.; acute sorrow; deep sadness." When we think of care-giving to people who are grieving, we usually think of the grieving process people go through when the death of a loved one or a similar ending to the quality of life has taken place. However, people experience grief from other experiences of life, which many times involves the continuation of living.

Ted, Alice, and their three children joined a local church. They appeared to be a good-looking and cheerful family. Ted was outgoing, as were their children, but Alice seemed to always remove herself from social get-togethers. Sure, she was pleasant enough when greeting others at church, but there seemed to be something missing in her demeanor. On one occasion, she hurried to the bathroom when they met someone from the town they had just moved from. It seemed that Alice did not want to get too close to people. She stayed at home all day, and from what Ted says, "She doesn't want to go out very much anymore." Is Alice "grieving"? She was experiencing the loss of long-time friends and people she worked with when they moved, as well as leaving their first home that they fixed up together. You bet she was grieving, and it was interfering with her quality of life and her relationships with her family, friends, and potential friends who wanted to get to know her.

I am sure that we all have experienced a similar type of grief like Alice had. True, it may not have been caused by a move to another city or state, but it may have been triggered by changing a job, losing a friend, or the intense loneliness or longing for someone who is absent. The absence of this "love object" is not readily replaced by someone or something new, and the process of grieving over the loss begins. In care-giving to people who are hurting with grief, here are some important points to remember:

1. View the situation from their point of view. It is important in developing of a trusting and understanding relationship that you view the situation from their point of view. Many times, people will get stuck in a whirlwind of emotions that do not make sense to you. "I wouldn't view it that way," you may think. "What in the world is wrong with this person. They are upset about something that I have to deal with every day." It doesn't really matter how you would deal with their situation, and the person who is hurting probably doesn't want to hear how bad you have it. What they do want and need is for you to understand. Understand that they are hurting. Understand that even though it may sound silly, it is important all the same. They want you to not only understand, but to accept them...grief and all...as a valuable person. If you are able to "walk a mile in their moccasins," you will go a long way in being able to help them heal. If you come to the session with a condescending attitude, a haughty demeanor, or speak to them in such a way that they feel belittled, you have lost them. They will not come to you for help, and may get the idea that you do not care and cannot help them when they need to talk to someone.

2. Allow them to talk. People who are hurting need to talk. It may take them a while to muster the confidence, trust and courage to utter to another person what is causing them so much pain, but talking is what they need to do. If you need to always take the spotlight, or if you believe that "what I have to say to them is more important than what they are babbling about," you (and they) lose! People love to talk about themselves. Your job as a caregiver is to give them the opportunity to express their thoughts and feelings openly. At times, you may have to "prod" them along when they seem to get stuck. "Tell me more about what you were feeling when..." "I remember something about the situation, but am not sure that I fully understand it. Could you bring me up to date...?" "It seems that you are very upset. Could you tell me what has happened since we last talked?" These are some of the statements you can use to "jump-start" a person who has difficulty communicating what they are experiencing.

3. Find out the significance of the love-object. Even though you may believe that the situation you are hearing is not a big deal, and you have had to be creative in jump-starting them to talk more, you need to find out what part this loss has played in their general quality of life. You may ask the person to tell you by asking: "Tell me Mr. _____, how does not having this (thing or person) affect your life now?" By striving to understand the situation from their point of view, you will probably soon understand the significance of this object.

4. Significance of object to person. As previously mentioned, let the person talk without your interjecting some "quick-fix, Band-Aid" verbiage. Ask probing questions that elicit more than a simple one or two word answer. You especially want to avoid questions that can be answered by a simple "yes" or "no" response. The reason you want to avoid these type of questions is that these answers do not give you much information. Asking questions are a way for you to better understand. They are also a way for the person to understand their situation from a new perspective. If you listen carefully, you will probably understand the significance of the love-object to the individual.

Everyone understands the type of grief that Alice had experienced; moving from a place where special memories were forged. Memories and special relationships were left behind when they moved to another city. Thankfully, these memories and relationships do not have to be something that was only once experienced, they can still be experienced, though in a different way, if time and creativity are expended in keeping up with people and visiting places. There is another type of grief that revisiting cannot take place to lessen its impact. That which we grieve over can only be revisited through our memory, for it is locked in our past. The grief that I speak of is when a loved one dies.

Over 22 years ago, Elisabeth Kubler-Ross identified stages people go through who have suffered a significant loss. This loss may be of a loved one who has died, or of a very special relationship with another person that has ended. Anyone who experiences a significant loss of any kind seems to go through the stages that Kubler-Ross identified. In her book, *On Death and Dying*, Kubler-Ross identifies the following stages:

1. Denial and Isolation

2. Anger

3. Bargaining

4. Depression

5. Acceptance

It is important to understand that every person does not start at number one. Nor does every person go through this progression in the order presented. For example, one person may start with anger, go to the depression stage, and so forth. Another person may start at the denial and isolation stage, skip the anger stage, and move right into the bargaining stage just before sinking into a deep depression. By being familiar with these stages, you will be able to identify and understand other emotions and "stages" the person who has suffered great loss will experience.

No pastoral ministry offers the open door of spiritual opportunity as does the presence of death in the church family. Death is so universal, its visage is so stark and grim, and its presence is so dark and dreaded. When death occurs, there are oceans of heartaches and rivers of tears. This is the hour when the loving and caring Christian caregiver is needed the most.

When death comes to a home, a Christian caregiver should be the first one there to strengthen the survivors in their hour of need. The problem can come when the caregiver has not themselves dealt with the death of a loved one. As a young pastor in a Southwest Virginia coal-mining community, I was called on to do many things. One day I was called to our local hospital to spend some time with a family that was hurting very deeply. The patriarch of this family, their spiritual leader was slowly leaving this world. One of the finest Christian men I have known was going to see his Savior. The issue was that brother Myers was ready, but this young preacher wasn't quite sure.

I left the family in a waiting area and went down the long hallway to his room. Thoughts, emotions, words, nothing seemed to focus for me. I was trained and educated in how to minister, what to say, how to give comfort, etc. But now, here I was with a friend, a deacon, a mentor, a brother in Christ. My stomach was churning. Brother Myers saw my state of utter confusion and simply said, "Preacher, it's going to be all right. Just sit here a while and read me some from your Bible."

The weight of the world was lifted. I began to read, "The Lord is my Shepherd" (Ps. 23). The next few minutes were special and all my training seemed to come into focus. I spent time with the family, and the memorial service was a time of comfort and blessing. God had shown me that He is truly able to give insight when the caregiver is willing. The point I learned was that even though I was trained and "educated" as to what to do, the most important part of this experience was my learning to listen to and follow the Lord's leadership. This is a very important ingredient for the care-giving ministry agenda. Even though you may have a lot of training in a particular area, you will never know enough to not listen to God's leading in each and every situation that He allows you to deal with. I believe that if we were to listen more to God's leading and direction, our lives would be much more productive both personally and professionally.

We have learned the following practical insights in dealing with this particularly important part of ministry...ministering to individuals experiencing grief from the death of a loved one.

Without question, losing a loved one can be one of the most traumatic experiences we face. Not only must we face the initial shock to the loss, but the after shock of the loss and the emptiness felt when the funeral cars have gone, and friends and well-wishers have left. For some, when this happens, a feeling of abandonment ensues. "No one comes by any more since my husband died," a widow may say. Another widower may lament that "people don't call or stop by like they did when Alice was alive." Because other people do not understand that a big part of bereavement is that the one who did not die feels all but dead to friends and other people.

For others, friends continue to stop by and get the person experiencing the loss of a loved one out and around. They call, they stop over, and they "aggressively" pursue the individual so that the person does not give up on living life because a loved one has gone to be with the Lord. You as a caregiver have a responsibility too. Consider the following areas and ask yourself, "Where do I line up with each of these areas?" If they bring about specific thinking about your values of life and death...GOOD! You may know where you stand and what you believe in your heart. No matter which of these statements you identify with, consider anew your beliefs as you read the following.

1. The caregiver must understand the nature of death.

2. The caregiver must understand his/her abilities to help in the time of bereavement.

3. The caregiver must understand that death, whether expected or unexpected, often is an emotional earthquake.

4. The caregiver must understand that his/her most important function is to just be there; not compulsively talking but sharing, caring, and being helpful. Our faith gives strength and support. Use prayer, the Bible, but most of all listen. Remember that this is not a time for judgment; God alone judges. It is not a time to preach a sermon; wait for Sunday or Wednesday! It is a time to be aware that death heightens your consciousness about your own mortality. Hebrews 9:27 says, "It is appointed unto men once to die."

5. We must remember that the funeral service does not draw the curtain on our emotions. The emotions and words spoken live long past the incident where they initially took place.

A woman whose husband died was heard to say, "If I had known ahead of time how desperately I would need help later, I would have replaced the guest book in the funeral home with a calendar, asking each visitor to designate a day in the future on which they would console me by way of a visit, a card or a phone call."[3]

In reality, the death and burial of a loved one is often tragic and hurts a lot. The most painful time though, in my opinion, is after everyone has left. Our most needed time of caring for others may be when the family and friends have left and the person we are seeing in our care-giving ministry is alone. Show the love of God in helping and in being there. Most of all, be there and listen. Listen not only with your ears, but "listen" with your eyes and heart. It is surprising how much more you can "hear" when you use your eyes than when you use your ears. Many times you will notice that a person's "actions" speak louder than their words.

FOOTNOTES

[1] Criswell, W.A. *Criswell's Guidebook for the Pastor.* (Broadman Press, Nashville, TN) 1980.

CHAPTER NINE

CHAPTER NINE
Crisis Counseling

Bob had been a successful businessman for a number of years. Helen, his wife, was a homemaker. Their three children were doing well in school. Bob and his family were active in a number of organizations in their church, and were known as a family who readily helped others in need. The news that Bob's company was having financial difficulty was not news to Bob who had worked in a technical position with his company for 17 years. But, the information that Bob received with his paycheck on the Friday before their 15th wedding anniversary was. He was being given a choice to take a drastic pay reduction or look for another job. Bob was distraught because of this sudden information. He and Helen had made "expensive" plans for celebrating their anniversary and their oldest child was to get braces very soon. They had many financial obligations which included a large amount they had prayed about giving to their church for the building fund. Now, all of this was evaporating in Bob's thoughts when he thought about the note he had gotten. He pondered what he would do, and how he would tell Helen. Before going home, he contacted his pastor who, along with a caregiver in their church, talked to Bob.

Bob, who had always been a careful planner and was able to see things beyond the present circumstances was now very confused and depressed. "My entire world is crashing down around me," he said. "And the worst part of it is that I can do nothing about it." This man, who had always been seen as a strong solid individual, was now very depressed and weakened. All of the ways that Bob had dealt with stressful situations in the past were not working now. He felt helpless, hopeless, and unable to deal with this crisis in his life. Now, Bob sat before his caregiver, wanting to know what he should do.

Before you tell Bob anything (or anyone else in a crisis situation for that matter), it is important to not only know *what* a crisis is, but also how you can help a person facing a crisis.

The word *crisis* comes from the Greek word *krisis*, which literally means "to separate." In medicine, the word describes the turning point of a disease. It also refers to a turning point in the course of most things that we experience in various experiences of life. Crisis has come to have a more emotional or psychological meaning than a physical one. It is usually used in connection with a radical change or event which is characterized by an unusual instability caused by some sort of excessive stress in a given situation. Many times, this stress is strong enough or lasts long enough to cause the individual experiencing it to feel endangered.

When we look at crisis situations that a caregiver may encounter, it is important to first understand what a crisis is before we can know what to do in this highly emotionally charged state. The Chinese word for "crisis" is made up of two characters, each of which have their own individual meaning. One of the characters means *danger* while the other character means *opportunity*. When these two characters are blended together, they form the word *crisis*.

The idea here is that a crisis presents both a *danger* and an *opportunity* to the person experiencing it. Crisis is a *danger* in that it can potentially threaten to overwhelm the individual or their family, and may result in suicide, physical harm, or long-lasting psychological damage. It is also, however, an *opportunity* to change, grow, and develop better ways of coping. As a caregiver, your timely and skillful intervention may not only prevent the development of a serious long-term disability, but may also allow new coping patterns to emerge that could help the individual you are dealing with develop a higher level of functioning and equilibrium than they had before the crisis.

As mentioned before in our definition of the word, a person experiencing a crisis is at a turning point in their life. They are faced with a problem that they cannot readily solve by using the coping mechanisms that have worked for them in the past. As a result, their tension and anxiety increases, and they become less able to find a solution, or a way out of their current crisis situation. When a person in a crisis situation comes to you, as a caregiver, they feel helpless to change, cope, or deal with their situation. They are caught in a state of great emotional unrest and they often feel that they are unable to take any action on their own to solve the problem.

How You Can Help

Understanding that a crisis presents both danger and opportunity is a tremendous benefit to you as a caregiver. It allows you to view the crisis situation as having a number of options for the individual experiencing the crisis. Rather than looking at the person's situation as only doom-and-gloom, you will be able to offer the person some rays of hope. Rather than the light at the end of the tunnel being a train, you can show the person that the light is actually a way out! In order for you to be effective as a caregiver, you will need to adopt a number of self-attitudes. From these attitudes of understanding your role come a number of questions that you will want to ask, and suggestions as to what you need to do to bring about change for the person experiencing a crisis.

1. Know what to do. Essentially view your work with the person in crisis as a short-term intervention with the goal of directing the tremendous amount of energy that is generated from the crisis. This is NOT the time to conduct long-term care-giving. Rather, it is very short in duration (or time spent) and is directed toward focusing the person's energy into something productive, or at least benign. With the heightened emotionalism that a crisis brings, it is easy for the individual experiencing it to do irrational things and think irrational thoughts. They do not act like themselves, they feel a great need to do something, but they (many times) do not know what they need to do! This is where you as a caregiver come in. You are the one to help direct the actions and plant ideas that will help the person successfully work through the situation. You are able to see clearly what steps, no matter how small at first, must be taken. And you can support their actions and suggest a plan for them to follow.

2. Assess the problem. In order to know what to tell the person who comes to you in crisis, you must first have an accurate assessment of the presenting problem. You need to know and understand what has happened, when it happened, who is involved, and who else needs to know before you can be helpful.

3. Help or help with referral. If the situation requires either extended, in-depth, or professional intervention, your job is to help the individual secure someone who can work with them. This does not limit your crisis intervention, rather it is an option that you can take once you have found out more information about the situation at hand. Most of the time, once you have found out what has happened and know what needs to be done, you will be able to better determine whether or not you are the one who should continue with the individual after the immediate crisis situation is over. If you have the time, and are qualified to do so, you can set up regular meeting times to get together. If you do not have the time, or if the individual is becoming "attached" to you because of your position, you should refer the individual to someone who is better able to meet the needs of the individual, in either time, duration or expertise.

4. *Keep focused.* It is important, when dealing with a crisis situation, to stay focused on the situation at hand. Many times an individual will talk about other issues that "may" relate to the topic at hand, or they may go off on related "rabbit trails" because their thinking during the crisis is scattered and illogical. You need to be alert to what they are saying, and strive to keep them on track when relating information that is important for your understanding of the situation.

5. *Get involved, and don't be afraid to do what needs to be done.* Crisis intervention, for the caregiver, is an active and sometimes directive role. You need to ask straight questions, be willing to confront walls of pride, and actively solicit information from the individual you are seeing and from significant others that are involved in the crisis. Waiting until it is convenient to talk to someone, or holding off asking a question because you believe that "this certainly could not apply to this person" won't work! You must be willing to do what is necessary, in a timely fashion, whether it is convenient or not. Remember that a crisis presents you with the responsibility to direct a lot of energy into doing something. Merely telling the person in crisis to "cool down" or "go home and pray about it" simply is not enough! You must be willing to get your hands dirty, get involved, and support the efforts of the individual you are helping.

6. *Stay flexible but strong.* It would follow then, that in order to be effective in your care-giving to people in crisis situations, that your approach must remain flexible. At times, you will wear different "hats." Sometimes, you will be called on to be a resource person or information giver. At other times, your role will take an active posture in establishing a liaison with other helping professionals or resources that would be more appropriate in their particular situation. Whatever role you take in helping someone through crisis, you need to develop and maintain a maximum flexibility of approach in your care-giving.

7. A specific goal. The goal in crisis intervention is very explicit. All of your energies, using the many "hats" of flexibility you may be called upon to employ, is directed entirely toward returning the individual to at least their pre-crisis level of functioning. In the case of Bob and Helen, your task would be to help Bob think out a step-by-step approach to solving this crisis situation concerning his job and other financial obligations. When Bob is able to talk through some options he has, he will be better equipped to talk with Helen, and develop a step-by-step plan to decide what he should do. He may well be able to remember what he has done in similar situations in the past and, with a little modification, employ similar coping patterns to deal with the task at hand.

Steps in Crisis Intervention:

As with any program, you will want to follow specific steps when dealing with a person who is in a crisis situation. These steps cannot really be put into clearly defined categories, but the steps you will take in helping someone in crisis would pass through the sequences listed below.

1. The first step is to accurately assess the individual and his/her problem. Stay focused on the individual you are helping so you can obtain an accurate assessment of the precipitating event that has caused the crisis, and the resulting circumstances that have brought the individual to you for help. Determine whether or not the individual seeking your help presents a high suicidal or homicidal risk. If you believe

the person *is* a high risk to himself or to others, re-ferhim or her to a professional or to a hospital for further evaluation. In the event that hospitalization is *not* needed, the crisis intervention continues. Keep in mind that a lot of time may be required to completely assess the circumstances related to the immediate crisis situation. To hurry someone in relating details and facts to you will send a message loud and clear that "you don't understand," and that "you really don't care about me."

2. The second step is to plan a therapeutic intervention. After you have accurately assessed of the precipitating event(s) of the crisis, plan an intervention. Basically, an intervention will help answer the question, "What do we do now?" Remember that this intervention is not designed to bring about major changes in the personality structure of the individual. It *is* designed, however, to restore the person to at least their pre-crisis level of equilibrium. It is important then, to determine the length of time since the onset of the crisis itself. Usually, the precipitating event has occurred from 1 to 2 weeks *before* the individual comes to you for help. Frequently though, it may have occurred within the past 24 hours!

Keep in mind the following questions and considerations in this second step:

* Know how much the crisis has disrupted the individual's life.

* Determine the amount of disruption the crisis has caused on the individual and on others in his/her environment.

* Seek to determine the individual's strengths.

* Find out what coping skills the individual may have already used successfully in the past and is not using presently.

* Secure other people in his/her life that might be used as a support for them.

* Begin to assist the individual in looking for alternative methods of coping, that for some reason they are not presently using.

3. The third step in the crisis process is the actual intervention. Morley (1967) suggests that some of the following intervention techniques have been found to be helpful. The real key to being successful in this intervention phase is your:

1. Pre-existing skills that you possess as a caregiver.

2. Creativity, not only in asking questions and eliciting accurate information, but also in ideas you present to those you are helping.

3. Flexibility in how you address the circumstances surrounding the crisis situation and people involved.

4. I would add, perhaps foremost, knowledge and practical application of the Scriptures to the person and their situation. "Shoving it down" a person's throat nor telling the person that the Bible says you should, should not, should not have, etc., is not what the person needs to hear. Rather accurately, lovingly, sympathetically and knowledgeably apply Scriptural truths to a hurting person and their situation, with the goal of restoration and healing.

   A. Help the individuals gain an intellectual understanding of their crisis. Many times an individual experiencing a crisis sees no relationship between a dangerous situation occurring in their life and the extreme discomfort they are experiencing. If you sense that this is taking place with the individual you are counseling, it may be best for you as a caregiver to use a more direct approach in making the connections between their crisis situation and the discomfort they are experiencing.

B. Help the individual bring into the open their present feelings. Frequently people suppress various feelings they have. This is also true for Christians, who may believe that it is wrong to have feelings of anger. Others may believe that it is "OK" to have the feelings of anger, but to admit to another that they have this or other inadmissible emotions is "simply not done." If this is the case, the caregiver must encourage the individual to express these emotions verbally. Even if these emotions are directed toward someone they feel they "should honor and love," their pastor, spouse, parent, child, etc., you should encourage them to verbalize their emotions.

A person may also experience a denial of grief, feelings of guilt, or an incompletion of the mourning process following a bereavement. Again, it is important for you to encourage them to express these emotions, verbally. The goal here is to reduce the tension experienced by the individual, by providing a means for the individual to recognize these feelings and bring them into the open. Once in the open, they can be dealt with. If they stay covered up inside the individual, they may never surface or be able to be recognized and healed.

C. Explore various coping mechanisms to assist the individual in looking at alternate ways of coping. If for some reason the behaviors used successfully in the past are not being used for this particular situation, look at the possibility of their implementation. Otherwise, new coping methods will need to be sought. Frequently, the person devises some highly original methods that they have never tried before. Since there is no reason to "reinvent the wheel," strive to find out what *has worked* in the past for them in similar situations. It is also important to ask and understand what has *not* worked in the past.

D. Reopening the social world. If the crisis has been precipitated by losing someone who played a significant role in the person's life, many people tend to shield themselves from other people. They do this by never getting with others, not calling friends, and not attending social and/or church gatherings. They may believe that being alone will be best, however, it can actually be the worst thing they could do! Introducing them to other people, encouraging them to get involved with others can be very supportive and healing. The caregiver may assist in this by offering to go with them to a function or coordinating other people to visit, call or go with them to different places (for more on dealing with grief, refer to Chap. 8).

4. The last phase in this process is resolving the crisis and anticipating plans. Reinforce the adaptive coping mechanisms that the individual has used successfully to reduce tension and anxiety. Give assistance to the individual on an "as-needed" basis. Some people will do most of this on their own once they feel that they are on more solid footing. Others will need help to put one foot in front of the other in their steps to healing.

In either case, help them make realistic plans for the future. It is also helpful to discuss ways in which the present experience (crisis) may help them cope with future crises better.

Your encouragement here should be very reality oriented. Focus on solving specific problems that arise from situational or interpersonal difficulties. You, as a caregiver, should have a greater knowledge of the situation surrounding the crisis than the person experiencing it. You should also be able to relate the reality of the Scriptures in a practical, supportive, healing fashion in the midst of a highly emotional situation.

An important principle to remember in helping a person through a crisis situation is that your job as a caregiver is to assist the individual in making choices. Notice that I have used the word "assist" and did not imply that you should make the decisions for them. True, if the person you are seeing is so incapacitated that they are unable to make initial decisions on their own, or if their decisions are clearly in violation of biblical principles or are dangerous to their own or other's health and safety, it may be better for you to decide what is best to do initially. However, if this is not the case, or when they are able to take more control, you will need to step back and allow them to make their own decisions.

Always reinforce the options that are available. Assist them by showing various options available to consider along with the practical consequences of each option you come up with.

After the crisis, if you begin to see that the person is depending on you too much, you may need to "wean" them from you. This should be done gently, but firmly. Frequently a dependence of this kind happens when a person is helped by a person of the opposite sex. Because a crisis tends to be a highly emotionally charged situation, and a person's cognitions (thinking) are *very distorted* during this time, unrealistic expectations and feelings may arise in either the caregiver *or* in the person getting help through their difficult time. Be on guard for dependence. Keep healthy boundaries and practices that will ensure safety for both you and the person you are helping. If you believe that the person you are helping is getting "too close," refer them to someone with more experience and training in the area of need that person has.

Sometimes a caregiver has such a need to be wanted and to help others that he or she starts to invade the person's space needed to develop options themselves. The following questions may help you honestly examine your motives and actions. The key is to know yourself well enough to answer honestly:

* "Why am I helping this person?"

* "Am I really qualified to give them the help they need in this situation?"

* "Are they getting more benefit from my helping them than I am?"

* "Is my helping this person fulfilling a need within me?" "What need is it fulfilling in my life?"

* "Am I able (or willing) to let this person work things out for themselves now that the crisis is over?"

By honestly answering these and other questions, you will likely find that you are helping yourself *and* the person who came to you with the crisis in their life. Ultimately, your goal is to reduce the symptoms of disequilibrium and to restore the individual to a pre-crisis level of functioning, with improved abilities to solve similar situations. Hopefully, they will also have a closer walk with God and a renewed appreciation for the power of God in their lives when applied in a practical and loving manner. Their ability to help others with similar situations will be a way that they can contribute to the overall health of the body of Christ.

The Bible and Crisis Types

Everyone has been told of the patience of Job. Usually this Bible story is told to us when patience is something we desperately need. We would like to be more patient, but most of us wish that God would "cover" us with this quality while we are asleep so that it wouldn't hurt too much. Then, when we awaken, we would be able to exude this quality in any situation it is needed. I have not heard of God developing this quality in people's lives this way, but I admit that it would certainly be easier if it were done this way!

If we were given various qualities while asleep, we would probably not appreciate them nearly as much if we did not have to "work" at developing them. Along with our lack of appreciation, we would most likely misuse these qualities to the point that no one would benefit from our having them.

This example is not just for the quality of patience. The Bible speaks of a number of qualities that are developed through crisis situations. In fact, much of the Bible deals with crisis. When we look through the Scriptures, we see that many familiar stories were wrought with crisis. Adam and Eve, Cain, Noah, Abraham, Isaac, Joseph, Moses, Samson, Saul, David, Elijah, Daniel, and a host of other Bible characters faced crisis in the Old Testament.

Jesus faced crises, especially at the time of the crucifixion (Matt. 27:11), as did the disciples (Acts 12), Paul (Acts 14:8-9), and many early believers (Acts 7:59-60). Several of the Epistles were written specifically, it seems, to help individuals or churches meet crisis situations. Hebrews 11, for example, summarizes what happens with a crisis that has a happy ending, and those that resulted in torture, incredible suffering, and even death.

As with most situations, once we know and understand what makes something up, it is easier to deal with. For example, trying to help someone who comes to you, stating that they have a "a lot of problems" is difficult. Once, however, you are able to break down these problems and understand what "a lot of problems" means, they are easier to deal with. The same is true with the topic of crisis. There are three different types of crisis that we face in life. Let's look at these three crisis types and identify them with examples from the Bible.

Stressful events that originate outside the family tend to solidify a family; things such as a natural disaster, a serious fire, racial prejudice, etc. This can clearly be seen historically with the early church. When under persecution from the Roman government, the church solidified and grew stronger. Not too many years ago, when Communism was a strong force in Russia, the underground church solidified and grew also. Similarly, when persecution happens outside the "family," the members tend to pull together to resolve the crisis. In doing so, the "family" usually becomes stronger.

When a crisis or stressful event happens inside the family, the family stands a good chance of tearing apart. A suicide attempt, infidelity, child abuse, drug abuse or alcoholism are but a few internal problems that can easily tear families apart. In the church, internal strifes, "cold-wars" between members or between one or two people and the leadership of the church, can also be a threat to the solidification and growth of the "family."

1. Situational or Accidental Crisis: This type of crisis occurs when a person's security is suddenly threatened, or an extremely disruptive event happens, such as a sudden death or unexpected loss. To add insult to injury is when crises come in sequence. When one crisis comes on the heals of another crisis, problems are intensified three-fold. This was Job's experience. Within a very short period of time, this godly man lost his family, his wealth, health, and status. His wife, who should have supported him, told him to curse God (Job 2:9). The "friends" who came around all the time when things were good, learned about Job's anger and inner turmoil and concluded that there must be some unconfessed sin in his life for all of this to have happened. Job must have been very confused as to why a loving, caring God would let so many bad things happen to him.

2. Developmental Crisis: This type of crises happens during the normal course of human or organizational development. I can remember when my daughter first started school, my wife and I were in a "developmental" crisis. When she goes away to college, we will be in another "developmental" crisis, I am sure. Some other common developmental crises we experience are marriage, the birth of a child, parenthood, declining years and old age, etc. Abraham and Sarah, for example, had to cope with a lot of developmental crises in their lives. Moving to a new land (Gen. 12:1-5), criticism from others, the many years of childlessness (Gen. 16:1), and various other family stresses. After the birth of their long-awaited son, Isaac, Abraham dealt with a tremendous crisis in his life when God commanded that young Isaac be sacrificed.

How about trying to raise a unique child like John the Baptist. This would try any parent. Think of it as if you were elderly like Zacharias and Elizabeth were (Luke 1:7). Even more unique, think of being the parents of Jesus. Think of the many things they must have encountered with raising a son so special and brilliant as Jesus. It seems to me that Mary and Joseph were really on the line when it came to being "good parents!"

3. The third type of crisis espoused by many contemporary writers is one that actually overlaps the other two. It is called **Existential Crisis.** The reason it overlaps the other two types of crisis is because in an existential crisis, we often face disturbing truths about ourselves. During these crises, thoughts come to us that are disturbing. They are sometimes thoughts that we have successfully tucked away for some time, but this particular situation or crisis brings them screaming to the forefront of our attention. Phrases like:

* I'm single again.

* I am a failure.

* I'll never be successful.

* My marriage is ending in divorce.

* People always treat me unfairly.

* I have nothing to believe in anymore.

* I'm too old to reach my life goals, etc.

These types of thoughts do not come "out of the blue" just because of the crisis at hand. No, these along with other similar realizations take time to grow. They take effort and an inward perspective over time to assimilate. They are very foundational to our self-image because they can produce changes in our self-perception. And, in order to have your life go on and be fulfilling, these thoughts cannot be denied any longer.

Elijah, after having a great spiritual victory (1 Kings 17:21), was chased by Jezebel and ran to the wilderness where he concluded that his life was a complete failure (1 Kings 19:4). In the midst of his struggles, Job must have wondered "What will happen next? What will become of me now?" Jonah probably had similar thoughts as he debated with God (Jonah 2).

When people ask you about the reasons for their crisis, it is difficult to and often (seemingly) impossible to give them definitive answers. Sometimes God does allow us to see the rhyme and reason for what happens, maybe not right away, but after a period of healing. But most times, the reason is not available to us while here on earth. Though the Bible speaks of these three types of crises, it does not give clear or complete reasons to totally explain why we suffer when and why we do. I have been asked by a mother whose son was electrocuted when trying to save an elderly couple that were trapped in a burning house, "Why did this happen? He was trying to help someone else live and he died. Why did this happen?" The only answer I could give at the time was "I don't know." If she were to come to me a year from now, I'm not sure I would have a better answer than what I told her soon after her son had died.

While we may agree that every event has a divine purpose and is therefore ultimately under God's control, it is still very difficult to give a specific reason that makes sense to someone who has experienced a tremendous loss. I do believe that crises can be a learning experience for us that can mold our character, and teach us about God like no other situation can. They can also teach us about God's resources, and can even stimulate us to grow and mature. But, the ultimate reasons for life's specific crises may never be known while we live on this earth.

A FINAL WORD

A FINAL WORD

The desire to begin a care-giving ministry in your church is not enough. You may have very good intentions and pure motives in your undertaking. But, without knowing basic principles from both the Scriptures and counseling, your efforts, as good and pure as they may be, fall short of the goal you have for providing help to others. The reason many people fail in this ministry is because they are not prepared. They do not know what they need to know to do the best job they can. When a care-giving ministry fails, it is usually not because motives were wrong for starting this ministry, and not because there was not enough prayer and consideration given to the subject. Rather, it may be that caregivers were not prepared in their knowledge (of self, others, and people in general), training, and understanding of what they needed to do to be ready. Many are willing to start or be involved in a care-giving ministry. Many believe that they can "talk to people," etc. But, *this is not enough!*

You, and the other caregivers who help in this ministry, must be the very best you can be. This involves a solid understanding and appraisal of self. It requires a Spiritual gift for this ministry, and educational background in dealing with people and their problems. It necessitates ongoing training in specific areas to equip the members of your care-giving "team" in knowing what to do and when to do it. And foundationally, it is imperative that each person has a solid relationship with Christ in such a personal way that it emanates from within, outward to others. If a person does not have that rock-solid relationship with God that filters all that they experience through Christ, then their views of how to help people with problems will (most likely) not honor

God. Your care-giving ministry needs to be built upon the solid foundation of the Word of God. The psychological and counseling techniques and principles do not have to run contrary to God's Word. In fact, they blend very well together. Our prayer is that this book will whet your appetite for learning more about this very important ministry. Investing in others through Christ can be very rewarding *if* you are led by the Holy Spirit and know what you are doing. You need *both!*

If your calling is there, your training and motivation to be the very best must be there also. If you have a strong calling but not much training, go to school. Take courses in subjects that will help you understand what you will need to know. If you have training but no calling, do not accept when asked to be a part of the care-giving team. If you have a calling from God to be a part of your church's care-giving team, you have been asked by your pastor, and you have the training and expertise (both formal and practical), then GO-FOR-IT. Once a caregiver in your church, further your education in various areas. Attend seminars, lectures, and workshops. Get involved with local counseling organizations so that you not only learn how to better meet other's needs, but you also develop a working relationship with other professionals in your community. You never know when that phone will ring and you will need to refer the counselee to someone else.

A care-giving ministry in your church can be the most beneficial ministry in your church. When you take the time to meet people's needs in their time of turmoil and trouble with good sound biblical truths and psychologically grounded principles, word will soon get around that your church really cares about people.

Not only do they say they care, they actually put their message into practice by meeting the personal needs people have. They have a specialized ministry with trained people who know how to deal with most any situation they come in contact with. They are people dedicated to God, and wise in both the Scriptures and educational training to meet the needs of people. And best of all, they do all of this in a practical, understandable manner!"

When you invest in people you invest in families. When you invest in families and meet their needs in their time of need, you build a strong and vibrant church. You cannot do it all by yourself. You will need help. Above all, you need help from God, but you also need the help of dedicated people who know what they are doing. The families you invest in will, in turn, invest in their church also. People want to be more than a number (whether it is how much they tithe or whether their presence adds to the total number in church today). They want to feel that they are a part of something that helps others. When they receive help in their time of need, they know that others can get help in their time of need also. People flock to people who care. Your ministry of care-giving is the vehicle that can bring others into your church for help, and keep families in your church when they need help. If someone else is investing in people's lives through the ministry of care-giving, people will seek *them* out.

SELECTED RESOURCES

Selected Resources

Baldwin, Carol Lesser, *Friendship Counseling*, Zondervan.

Briscoe, D. Stuart, *Tough Truths for Today's Living*, Word.

Collins, Gary R., *Called to Joy: A Design for Pastoral Ministries*, Convention Press.

Collins, Gary R., *Christian Counseling*, Word.

Collins, Gary R., *How to Be A People Helper*, Regal.

Collins, Gary R., *Innovative Approaches to Counseling*, Word.

Hightower, James E., *Called to Care: Helping People through Pastoral Care*, Convention Press.

Search, (Fall 1992). Publication of The Sunday School Board of the Southern Baptist Convention in Nashville, Tennessee.

Sturkie, Joan & Bear, Gordon R., *Christian Peer Counseling*, Word.

Sturkie, Joan & Tan, Siag Yang, *Peer Counseling in Youth Groups*, Zondervan.

Tan, Siag Yang, *Lay Counseling*, Zondervan.

Wright, Norman, *How to Get Along with Almost Anyone*, Word.

ORDER FORM

Quant.	Item #	Product Name	Price per Item	Total	Info. only (No charge)
	427T	*Counseling: Offering a Needed Touch in Times of Trouble* textbooks	8.95		☐
	427	*The Complete Guide to Starting a Local Church Counseling Ministry* resource packet	79.95		☐
	427L	*Local Church Counseling Ministry* **lapel pins** 25-49 pins, .85 ea.; 50-99, .75 ea.; 100 or more, .70 ea.			☐

Shipping

up to $3.00: **$1.00**
$3.01 to $20.00: **$2.50**
over $20.00: **$5.50**

Outside USA:
Add **$1.00**
to above charges

TOTAL ORDER [ ]
Shipping (see chart) [ ]
Amount Enclosed [ ]

Method of Payment:
☐ Bill Church (established accounts *only*)
☐ Check/M.O. Enclosed ☐ VISA ☐ MasterCard

Credit Card Account # [| | | | | | | | | | | | | | | |]

Cardholder Signature _____ Exp. Date _____

NOTICE CONCERNING PRICES The prices shown here reflect the prices at the time this text was printed. Since our resources are printed in bulk and placed in inventory, and prices are subject to change over time, the current prices may differ from what is listed here. Please confirm the prices at the time you order.

Check One:

☐ Pastor ☐ Youth Pastor ☐ C.E. Director ☐ Layperson ☐ S.S. Teacher

Name _____ Church _____

Address _____ City _____

State _____ Zip _____ Phone _____

Payment must accompany order
unless your church has an established account with Church Growth Institute.

Send order to:

Please allow 2-3 weeks for delivery.

9/93

Church Growth Institute
Providing Practical Tools for Growth
P.O. Box 4404, Lynchburg, VA 24502